Not My Will

Not My Will

Andrew Murray

Translated from the original Dutch by
Marian M. Schoolland

ZONDERVAN
PUBLISHING HOUSE
OF THE ZONDERVAN CORPORATION | GRAND RAPIDS. MICHIGAN 49506

NOT MY WILL

Copyright © 1977 by The Zondervan Corporation
Grand Rapids, Michigan

Library of Congress Cataloging in Publication Data
Murray, Andrew, 1828-1917.
   Not my will.

   Translation of Niet mijn wil.
   1. Christian life.   2. God — Will.   I. Title.
BV4501.M797613   248'.4   77-23137
ISBN 0-310-29722-2

Printed in the United States of America

83 84 85 86 87 88 — 10 9

Contents

Preface

In the will of God lies the origin of all creation — its very existence, its joys, its power, its glory.

In the will of God lies the origin of redemption — the fact of it, its power, its glory.

In the will of God alone lies the origin of grace in the life of each of His children — its being, its power, its blessedness, its glory.

Only in understanding and loving His will, in doing and enduring it, can that life of grace grow and find its rest, its joy, its strength, its fruitfulness, its blessedness. To live within the will of God is of primary importance to the Christian.

Whether it be the providential will of God or His will in the realm of grace, whether it be God's will as expressed in His commandments or as revealed in His promises, he who finds his very life in doing the will of God will find God Himself and the full blessedness of His presence.

May the Lord sanctify this little book to the end that His children will come to understand what God's will is, attain an insight into the glory of it, love it and choose it, and find that the doing of it is their highest delight.

ANDREW MURRAY

Wellington, South Africa
August 25, 1896

Prayer

O my Father, there is a word in Your precious Book about which I understand so little: *The will of God!* I know that Thy will is the glory of heaven, that there Thy will is supreme and all do Thy will. I have seen that in the doing of Thy will Thy Son was perfect. I have heard the voice of Thy Spirit in Thy Word, calling me to do Thy will even as it is done in heaven.

Lord, I understand so little of Thy will. I humbly plead, Teach me to know and to do Thy will. Truly, I am wholly Thine; I have given Thee my all, that I may no longer live according to my will but according to Thine. I pray, teach me to so know and love Thy will that I will obey it gladly.

Bless me also in the reading of this book, that it may help me day after day to live and to walk within Thy will, through my Lord Jesus Christ. Amen.

1

The Will of God – the Glory of Heaven

Thy will be done in earth, as it is in heaven (Matt. 6:10).

The Lord Jesus became man in order to do the will of God, and also to teach us to do His will, that we may live a heavenly life here on earth. He presents heaven as a place where the bliss consists in doing the will of God joyfully and always. He taught us to pray and to truly desire that His will may likewise be done on earth.

The Lord has shown me that one reason why many Christians are weak and often live in darkness is simply that they do not know how blessed it is to do the will of God. He has laid it upon my heart to tell them, as if it were a great secret, that if they will give themselves wholly to know and do the will of God, their darkness and their sadness will be turned into light and joy. I am inviting all to join me in these meditations, to listen to what God would teach us about this matter.

The invitation is for all. If you, my dear reader, are still living in sin and in worldliness, pause for a moment while

I tell you this: *God expects you to do His will.* You were placed in the world for that purpose. God has a right to require this of you. And God is worthy, unspeakably worthy, that you should seek to please Him by doing His will. It is the only sure way to happiness. No one can ever experience heaven, either now in his heart or hereafter, except in the will of God. Be quiet for a moment, then, and ask: *Have I ever said to my Creator, "Lord, Thou hast a right to ask it; I want to do Thy will in everything"?*

It may be that you are a young Christian, or a weak one. Perhaps you cannot understand why you make so little headway. I should like to show, from the Word of God, that it is simply because you have not yet given yourself wholly to do His will. When the tempter wanted to implant into Eve's mind the idea that it was unfair of God to forbid them to eat of all the trees, he awakened doubt by asking, "Has God said?" The same tempter entices us to doubt and to sin by suggesting: "Has God said? Has He strictly forbidden you to do what you would like to do? Has He said that you may never follow the leanings of your own will but must always do His?" That suggestion is truly a temptation spawned in hell. The will of God is nothing less than divine love and heavenly bliss. Let us believe this. Let us completely commit ourselves to God's will, declaring it to be our joy and life, always and in everything.

In the perfect prayer that He taught us the Lord seeks to awaken this desire in us. Man is motivated and driven by his desires. Without strong desire we never overcome any difficulties. The Lord Jesus tells us to desire the will of the Father, the will that is done in heaven and makes heaven so blissful, the will of God that can be done on earth. Thus we become like those in heaven. Set your heart on it, long for it, and pray, "Thy will be done, as in heaven, so on earth."

This prayer, once you have learned to pray it from the depths of your heart, can begin to fill your whole life. For prayer not only has power with God in heaven, it also affects our hearts. Prayer strengthens desire; it stirs hope for an answer and causes the soul to wait for it. It impels us to look for an answer in our own doing of His will. The will of God is the center of the universe, the pivot about which all things revolve and which upholds all. Earnest prayer makes the will of God central in our hearts; it upholds us and directs us; it renews and glorifies us, making us pleasing to Him.

O Christian, have you already chosen the will of God as your portion, your treasure, your delight? If not, join me in these meditations and learn how to pray this prayer in such a way that God can give you the complete answer: *His will within you now, on earth, as in heaven.* Begin today to let His will take possession of your heart. God wills to give Himself to you. By way of His will, God and heaven enter your heart; allow God and His will to fill it. Doing His will from the heart will make your life a heavenly life.

2

Doing God's Will – the Way to Heaven

> Not everyone that saith unto me, Lord, Lord, shall
> enter into the kingdom of heaven; *but he that doeth the will of
> my Father* which is in heaven (Matt. 7:21).

Every kind of tree grows in its own unique climate.
Every animal lives in its own element. A fish cannot live
on land; four-footed animals do not fly; birds cannot exist
under water. So too, the soul of man has a unique envi-
ronment where it feels comfortable and at home. There
must be compatibility between creature and environ-
ment. We have noted that the glory of heaven is God's
will; heaven is no less than the full domination of God's
will; heaven's citizens find complete joy in contemplating
and doing the glorious will of God. It goes without saying,
therefore, that the necessary preparation for heaven is the
doing of God's will. For no one can enter heaven unless he
has learned to do God's will.

Many people have a far different idea. They suppose
that prayer and worship, clean living and good works will

12

prepare them for heaven. Our Lord has assured us that this is not true. He contrasts the two ways plainly: "Not everyone who says to me Lord, Lord, shall enter the kingdom of heaven, but *he that doeth the will of my Father* who is in heaven."

Every created thing has an external appearance or form by which it is visible to us and also an internal power or life that is the essence or being of the thing. That is also true of heaven and of our ideas about heaven. We imagine a place of brightness and joy and glory where anyone would love to be. But many never stop to think that the essence of heaven's glory is the presence of "our Father who is in heaven" and the absolute sway of His will. They hope to go to heaven, though they are not at all fit for it because the desire and joy of their heart is not the Father in heaven and His will.

As there are two ideas about the way to heaven, there are also two about worship. For many, worship is merely outward form: prayer, Bible reading, church attendance, good works. They cry, "Lord, Lord," with great earnestness and reverence; they trust that the Lord Jesus will bring them to heaven. But the essence, the heart of worship — *to know and love and do the will of the Father* as their chief joy — to this they are strangers. It has never occurred to them that without this one cannot enter the kingdom of heaven.

If one should tell them so, they comfort themselves with thoughts of God's mercy. Did not the Lord Jesus come for just that purpose, to save sinners, those who have not done the will of God?

Yes, indeed. But they forget that He saves men only by first changing them, by giving then a new nature, so that even while they are on earth they learn *to love and do the will of God*. There is no possibility of entering heaven without that. The Lord has said plainly that those who *have done* the will of His Father in heaven shall enter the kingdom of heaven.

Let us take this to heart. May everyone grasp it: Life in

heaven, and the evidence on earth of fitness for such life, is *the doing of God's will*. And let us ask ourselves, "Is this evidence in my life? Is it this that I have committed myself to? that I long for and ask of God each day? Is *the will of God* my supreme desire, my greatest joy?"

I fear that there are many Christians who must admit: "No, it isn't." I fear that many Christians are deceiving themselves, hoping to enter heaven *without doing the will of the Father in heaven*. And this can never be. The Lord Jesus said it plainly: "Not everyone . . . shall enter into the kingdom of heaven, but they that do the will of my Father, who is in heaven."

Does this disturb you? Then do not delay. Turn to Him who said it in love. Turn to Him now. Tell Him that you are willing to learn the will of the Father and to do it. Tell Him that from now on you want to make this the rule of your Christian life: I will to do the will of the Father in heaven in all things. This is the only way to heaven.

3

Doing the Will of God – Our Oneness With the Lord Jesus

For whosoever *shall do the will of my Father* which is in
heaven, the same is my brother, and sister, and mother
(Matt. 12:50).

Have we learned the first two lessons well, so that we
know them? The first was: *The will of God* — the glory of
the heavenly life. And the second, similar to it: *Doing the
will of God* — the only way to enter heaven. Let us earnestly pray the Holy Spirit so to work in our hearts that
every thought of heavenly joy and every desire to have a
share in this joy may be permeated with the realization
that, whether in heaven or on earth, true joy is to be found
only in *living the will of God*. The closer to God's will, the
greater the joy. He who holds fast to this learns to give up
everything just to remain within that will.

We have come to our third lesson: Doing God's will is
the bond that makes us one with the Lord Jesus. Jesus
speaks of His brothers and sisters as people who have one
and the same Father with Him, who have the same

heavenly origin and nature. And what is the essential characteristic of this new nature that they have in common with Him? It is this, that they, like Him, live to do God's will. He came into the world not to do His own will, but to do God's will. This is the Spirit He breathes into His own; this is what it means to be like Him. They who do the Father's will are His brothers and sisters. They all have one Father; they have one Spirit; they have one will. To be one in will with the Father is the outstanding characteristic of the "Firstborn" and also of all His brethren.

Do you long for closer fellowship with the Lord Jesus? You sigh because you do not experience His nearness. You ask how you may come to assurance of His love and how you may know that He calls you by name, He sees you, He cares for you as for His own brother or sister. You have sought assurance by pondering and meditating. You have hoped to discover it in feelings of happiness. Or you have tried in vain to attain it through worship or activity in the church. You did not know that it is a matter of the will. It is in His will that I can find God. It is by absorbing His will into mine and doing it that life and blessing come. To love the Father's will, deliberately choose it, learn to know what it is and do it — that is the way to promote fellowship with Jesus. He came to do the will of God and to teach us to do it. The sacrifice of the human will and the commitment of it to the will of God, is the fundamental characteristic of the Son of God and also of all His brothers. "He who does the will of God is my brother, my sister. . . ." He and I share one life, one spirit, one love.

These words of the Lord Jesus shine into our hearts like a searchlight. Is our relationship to the Lord Jesus really grounded on this one great principle: to do the will of God? — not merely to wish or even pray that His will be done, but *to do* it? Is His will so holy, so glorious and precious to us that we are willing to sacrifice our own will completely in order to do His? Is this truly the blessedness

16

and joy that we experience in the Lord Jesus? Or, to make the question even more pointed: Is the doing of God's will truly the goal of my life, every day, so that I desire it as my highest joy? Read the question again and let your soul answer whether or not this is so. I once heard a godly missionary tell of his conversion and testify that it helped him greatly to say to himself each morning, "Today I will try to do God's will in everything until noon." Well, he who seeks that in the morning will soon learn to do it all day and every day.

O my God, make clear to my eyes, I pray, this secret of true union and fellowship with Thy dear Son. He lived only to do Thy will. That was His highest glory; that accomplished our salvation; and it is for this end that He lives in our hearts. Father, I profess to be Thy child, too — a brother or sister of Jesus Christ! Awaken in me the same desire, so that I may live as a brother or sister of the Lord Jesus, that Thy will may move me, that throughout my life I may ask nothing more than to do the will of my Father. Amen.

4

The Will of God: That the Perishing May Be Saved

Even so *it is not the will of your Father* which is in heaven, that one of these little ones should perish (Matt. 18:14).

Our Lord uses the words *little ones* not only in reference to the children about whom He had spoken (vv. 3-5) but also to "the little ones that believe on me," the lowly, who hardly count among men. And He says that as a man will seek a lost sheep and rejoice when he finds it, even so *it is not the Father's will* that one of these least should be lost. When Jesus talked about doing the Father's will, He meant that will especially as it concerns the salvation of the lost. "I came down from heaven," He says, "not to do mine own will, but the will of him that sent me. And this is *the Father's will* . . . of all which he hath given me I should lose nothing. . . . And this is *the will of him that sent me,* that everyone which seeth the Son . . . may have everlasting life" (John 6:38-40). His coming from heaven, His life on earth, every aspect of His obedience, and His holiness — all of these had but one purpose: to fulfill the will of God

18

regarding the salvation of sinners.

How about us? If we have committed ourselves to do the will of God, must the salvation of sinners be of prime importance to us, too? Or is the will of God for us found only in what the law requires, a life of righteousness and holiness? Surely not! The will of God as revealed in Jesus Christ is far broader and richer than the law, which was added because of sin till the promised Seed should come (Gal. 3:17,19). We may not let our selfish desires limit the will of God to what we think is necessary for our salvation. Genuine love for the will of God becomes evident in a willingness to see how very broad it is, in a desire to let as much as possible of it into our hearts and lives, in the commitment of our lives to the will of God concerning the salvation of sinners.

May everyone who sincerely prays, "Thy will be done!" receive into his own heart the loving will of God. Let us not deceive ourselves by thinking that the will of God consists of a few commandments. His will is far more glorious than that! It is the very nature of God, the revelation of His divine perfection, the expression of His limitless love. How foolish even to think of doing His will unless I have something of this great love in my heart! Therefore, we must open our hearts and allow the love of God to be poured in by the Holy Spirit.

May we come to realize that love for the lost is a most glorious aspect of God's will. May we recognize that love for the lost is one of the clearest evidences of true godliness, and a sure way to the full joy of salvation. Let us continue to pray earnestly, then, that God will fill our hearts with this love of His. Love for the lost is too often looked upon as something exceptional, but be assured that it is God's will for every one of His children; it is an indispensable part of your spiritual life.

Just like a man who seeks a lost sheep until he finds it and then rejoices over it, *even so* it is the Father's will that not one be lost. And *even so* it must be your will and your joy. God's will must be your will. His will moved Him to send His Son, to give His all. His will must move us to give all that we have, our very lives, for the salvation of the lost. Once this will has taken possession of our heart, it will move us to ask what can be done for the lost around us; it will make us willing, even compel us, to give ourselves wholly to prayer and supplication, to watch and to work, that souls may be saved. The will of God for the salvation of men shall become our joy.

You who profess to desire to do the will of God in everything, this is what you ought to pray for and seek. Plead with God to open your eyes. God's will is love for the lost. Tell Him that you live to do His will; offer yourself to Him to be filled with His love; and begin to reach out to those who are in need. The will is divine; the task is heavenly; you cannot do it. But if you make a beginning, God will work in and through you. He will work within you a divine willingness and in the strength of His love you will be able to work. And you will experience the truth of the Lord's promise even while you are still here below: "He that doeth the will of my Father which is in heaven, shall enter into the kingdom of heaven." For to do God's loving will is to live a heavenly life.

5

I have meat to eat that ye know not of. . . . My meat is *to do the will* of him that sent me, and to finish his work (John 4:32,34).

Jesus told His disciples that He had food to eat about which they knew nothing. It was heavenly food, unknown on earth and beyond human understanding. He also promises to give to His own the hidden manna, bread from heaven, that the world does not see or know of. This food is *the will of God*. Even as eating our daily food strengthens the body, doing the will of God makes the inward person strong.

Most Christians cannot understand this. To them, the doing of God's will seems a heavy burden, difficult and exhausting. They prefer to think of the promises of God and the life of Jesus as the food that strengthens them. They fail to see that *the will of God* is the power that upholds the universe, was so gloriously wrought in Christ, and is also at work in us through the indwelling of the

21

Spirit. The will of God is not intended to be a yoke laid on us, an oppressive burden. If it seems so to us, we are still under the law, living in the spirit of bondage. But if we have begun to walk by the Spirit of God and we too have the law of God written on our hearts, then the will of God becomes our joy. We want it and our hearts grow hungry for it, just as we hunger for food. Then we will sing, as David did, that the testimonies of God are sweeter than honey and the honeycomb.

We all know what it means to eat. The body cannot maintain itself independently; it must depend on things outside itself and take from the earth what is necessary to support life. Neither can our spirit support itself. For the support of our spiritual life we must receive food from the invisible world; we must eat heavenly bread.

Such eating is not, as many seem to think, accepting God's Word. We may ponder that Word, consent to it, hold to it, and delight ourselves in the knowledge of it; but that is of little avail. It does not feed the soul, *until we do it*. My food is *to do* the will of Him that sent me. I may accept the Word, but as long as I fail to do it, it remains outside of me; I have taken it into my mind, but not into my will and my life. The will of God is nourishing heavenly food that I need every day; I take it into my innermost self *by doing it*. The will of God is food that keeps our spiritual life alive.

Food gives us strength. We do not eat merely to stay alive. No, food renews life and increases vitality. We eat to be healthy and vigorous.

Even so, the doing of God's will not only serves to reassure us that we will live forever, it automatically makes for strong life; it increases vitality. Each act of obedience to the will of God makes a person stronger. This accounts for the great difference between a weak and a strong Christian. The weak person is the one who seeks peace and joy and bliss; to him doing the will of God is a *means* to attain this end. The strong Christian is one who knows that all things must be subject to the will of God and who makes the doing of His will his chief aim in life.

His one purpose and his joy is to discover the will of God and do it. He knows that when he does the will of God, he is, as the Scripture says, eating "the bread of heaven" (Ps. 105:40), the bread that God's servants in heaven eat, the bread that the Son of God ate when He was on earth. This is the food that makes one strong, a food that can be enjoyed every day.

We need food for our bodies daily. The will of God can be our spiritual food every day, and every hour, a food of which the world is unaware but which nourishes for eternal life.

We know that food tastes best when we are hungry. Make sure, then, that you have *a keen appetite for the will of God.* Hunger is stimulated by hard work and by the sight of food. Begin to do the will of God insofar as you know it. That will rouse greater desire to do it. Work stimulates appetite. Consider the will of God in all its perfection and glory; ponder the blessedness of having your will at one with His, of knowing that you are actually performing the will of God here on earth, until your hunger is stimulated to the highest degree and *nothing can satisfy you except to do His will always.* Then you can truthfully say, with the Lord Jesus, "My meat is to do the will of him that sent me, and to finish his work" (John 4:34). Then you will understand the beatitude "Blessed are they which do hunger and thirst after righteousness, for they shall be filled" (Matt. 5:6).

6

Sacrificing My Own Will

> I seek *not mine own will*, but *the will of the Father* which hath sent me. For I came down from heaven, not to do mine own will, but *the will of him* that sent me (John 5:30; 6:38).

Did Jesus then have a will of His own, different from that of His Father, that He should say, *"Not* my will"? Did He have a will that had to be denied? Undoubtedly, yes.

The crown of creation was just this that man had individuality, personality, a will of his own by which to govern his actions and choose what he should be. Having desires and longings and a will of his own was not sinful. Without these he would not have been a rational being. He had a will with which he had to decide whether or not he would live according to God's will. Sin entered only when man set his own will over against the will of God. And as a human being, like us in all things, the Lord Jesus also had His human will — to choose when to eat, for example, or whether to escape suffering. His perfect obedience consisted of His complete submission of His will to that of the Father. "I seek not my will, but the will of him that sent me."

For this, Jesus became man. By doing this He wrought redemption.

Man's seeking and doing his own will, in opposition to the will of God, is the root of all sin. The Lord Jesus came to free us from self-will. He, the Creator, became a creature, to teach us how necessary and how blessed it is to sacrifice our will to God's. He demonstrated for us that *absolute harmony with the will of God* and a life of complete submission to Him is the way to His glory. In fact, the submission of His will to the will of the Father is essentially His redemptive work. This is what made His death and atonement meaningful, gave it value. And this is the secret of His being our example. It is what He desires to work in us by His Spirit — *not my will, but the will of the Father.* He did not merely set us an example by His life and His death, but now that He is in heaven, it is still the main purpose of His work within each of His redeemed ones.

Dear reader, is this the Christ you have found? the Christ you love? the Christ who has as motto for His friends as well as for Himself: *The will of the Father always and in everything?* Are you sure you are not mistaken about your relationship to Him? Many think they can trust Him and go right on living according to their own desires. They have never yet said, "Lord God, I would live for Thee, in Thy Son and as Thy child; and like Him I say: Never, even in the least thing, must I want to have my own way; in the greatest and the smallest things, it is my desire to say: *The will of God* is what I want to do; I have been born again not to do my own will but the will of Him who saved me."

You may hear someone say, "But God gave man a will; surely man may make choices. To ask him to give up his will is to humiliate him, to deprive him of his independence and his personality." But did Christ — or did Paul — lose his personality? We forget who God is and how much He means to us. Does a child lose his personality by submitting himself to the will of a wise father? Surely not. By submitting his will to his father's, he learns to control it, to master it, to use it well. Neither is it a loss, but rather a rich gain, for one to surrender his will completely to God's. It is the glory of God to work for our good in everything. And it is the glory of man to serve God in everything, to know His will and do it. Surely, you can see that this is what makes man an image, a likeness, of God — surrendering himself so fully to God that God can do His will in him. There can be no greater honor or greater satisfaction than to do God's will.

Christ came to reveal this truth to us by His life, to deliver us from self-will by His death, and to implant in us a consuming desire to do God's will by sending His Spirit from heaven to teach us "the mind of Christ." Dear reader, is this the Christ you have come to know? Have you this Christ in your heart — the One who teaches you to say, *"Never, nowhere, and in nothing will I seek my will; in everything I will do the Father's will"*? Tell Him so; tell Him that you want to learn this from Him. Cling to Him. Trusting Him completely, dare to say, "In nothing will I seek my will; in everything I will do God's will." He who can sincerely say that will surely be taught by Him.

7

Doing God's Will – the Way to Spiritual Enlightenment

> If any man will do his will, he shall know of the doctrine, whether it be of God (John 7:17).

There was much doubt and a great deal of difference of opinion among the Jews about Jesus. "And there was much murmuring among the people concerning him: for some said, He is a good man; others said, Nay, but he deceiveth the people" (John 7:12). "And many hearing him were astonished, saying, From whence hath this man these things?" (Mark 6:2). They did not know what to think of Him. Much that He said about Himself, as the Son of the Father, was too exalted and unbelievable. How could they find out if what He said was actually true? The answer to this question and to many other questions about things that we find hard to believe is given to us in these words of the Lord: "If any man will do His will, he shall know of the doctrine whether it be of God."

In saying this, the Lord placed two things side by side: the will of God, which we must do, and the teachings of

27

God, which we must know. The teachings that come from God are often exalted and difficult to understand; the will of God expressed in His commandments is much easier to know and understand. The Lord says that if one is willing and truly sacrifices his own will *to do the will of God* insofar as he knows it, he will certainly be taught of God how to find out whether the doctrines of Jesus come from God. The doing of God's will is the sure path to the further guidance of God. There is a depth of meaning in this truth, and it has great bearing on our spiritual life. Let us see what we can learn from it.

1. The Lord teaches us that faith is dependent on one's walk. The reason many people cannot believe is that they are not willing to do God's will. Let this lesson sink into your heart: He who wills to do God's will will know that the teaching is from God. When the heart has determined to do God's will, the mind is made sensitive, ready to receive the teaching of God's Spirit. By accepting God's will as my will I draw nearer to God and He can bless me. We read of some who have "put away" their good conscience, not having kept it by doing the will of God, and consequently have suffered shipwreck of their faith. Faith depends on one's walk. If I lose my good conscience, I lose the power to believe.

2. God judges our walk according to our will. The Lord says, "If any man *will* to do [God's] will. . . ." That is, if one has set his heart on it, has truly made it his choice, God will bless him with further light on his way. It may be that someone has not yet made much headway in living according to the will of God because of ignorance or weakness, but if he truly wills to do God's will, he receives a blessing from God. "If there be first a willing mind, it is accepted according to that a man hath, not according to that he hath not" (2 Cor. 8:12). Therefore, we may fully expect blessings from God, even though we are keenly aware of our shortcomings, if we can honestly say, "He knows that I *will* to do His will with all my heart" — if we know that He sees our willingness to sacrifice all for it.

28

3. The way to do God's will is first of all to absorb that will into our own. My will is like an empty vessel that has no worth until the right content is poured into it. If I allow it to be filled with God's will, the content is heavenly; I have heavenly treasure in an earthen vessel. Before I even have the strength to do His will, I can choose it and cherish it, take it into my heart, and love it. He who does that and then makes every effort to do the will of God will be given the strength to do it. Willing leads to doing; the will of God has divine power.

4. Willingness to do God's will is the sure way to spiritual light and growth. TheLord Jesus assured the Jews of this: "If anyone wills to do God's will, he will know the divine nature of My teachings." Deeper insight into the Word of God, enlightenment of our minds by the Spirit, progress in spiritual growth — all of these depend on the sincere surrender of one's will to the will of God. On the other hand, dimness of faith, weakness, failure to grow spiritually — all these are caused by lack of sincerity in really willing to do the will of God in all things. There is one sure way to powerful spiritual living: become one with the will of God; learn to *will* His will. His blessing will certainly come upon you.

Let each one search his heart and ask, "Have I really grasped this great truth, that the beginning of the Christian life and the assurance of healthy spiritual growth are entirely dependent on complete surrender to the will of God — on my wholehearted desire to do that will and my sincere effort to do it?" If you have not, pray that the Spirit may make you keenly aware of this. And, trusting Him to help you, tell Him that you have decided: *"My will is to do God's will* in all things."

29

8

Thy Will Be Done!

> And he . . . kneeled down, and prayed, saying, Father, if
> thou be willing, remove this cup from me: nevertheless *not
> my will, but thine, be done* (Luke 22:41,42).

Gethsemane! the holy-of-holies in the life of our Lord,
the sanctuary of His eternal redemption, in some respects
more amazing to me than Golgotha. For the visible sacrifice on Golgotha was the external consummation of the
soul struggle that took place in Gethsemane. Gethsemane
reveals to me what happened between the Father and the
Son, the price the Son had to pay, and what it is that gave
His sacrifice its infinite worth. At the center of all this is
the word we are trying to understand: *"not my will!"*

Hush, my soul. Ponder and pray as you watch what
happened when your Savior Himself learned to say these
words in order to teach them to you in turn. Here we will
see four of the greatest marvels of all eternity.

The first is this: The Father offers His Son the cup of
wrath to drink. It is startling to note that the Bible speaks

30

of only two cups. There is the cup of blessing or thanksgiving (Pss. 16:5; 23:5; 116:13; 1 Cor. 10:16) and there is the cup of trembling or desolation (Ps. 11:6; Isa. 51:17,22; Ezek. 23:33). It is the Father's will that the Son drink this cup if he would make reconciliation for our sins. The Father places the cup of His wrath against sin in the hand of His Son.

The second marvel is that the Son, though always obedient, must now taste and empty the cup of the accursed death of sinful men.

He pleads that He may be spared the drinking of this cup. He experiences the revulsion of His human will and feels that His will is not the Father's will; He dreads death. But He dreads even more to be disobedient, and even while He says, *"Not my will,"* the struggle causes Him to sweat great drops like drops of blood.

The third marvel: The Father does not grant the request of the Son or do His will. It is not the Father's will that the cup should pass by.

The fourth marvel: The Son accepts the cup, so repugnant to His perfect soul; He sacrifices His own will. He rises and goes His way to do the Father's will, to drink the cup to the last drop, even to being forsaken of God.

All these marvels center about the words *"not my will."* That was what the Father wanted of the Son. That is what made the Son so glorious in God's sight. Self-will was the one root of all sin; only "not my will" could overcome and vanquish sin. Only this could open the way and show us the way back to God: that, regardless of the cost, a man should at last say, *"Not my will."* Jesus said it all through His life, day after day. And, thank God, He triumphed in the final test in Gethsemane and so assured us salvation.

"Not my will!" Those words are the secret, the key, of our salvation. In those three words the obedience of Jesus became the power for the atonement of our sins. Because of these words, all the sins of our self-will can be forgiven forever; in the balance they far outweigh all the self-will by which we have angered God.

And now those same words have become life for our souls. What constituted the power of redemption in Christ is also our source of power. We have been crucified with Christ; we share His willingness to bear the cross; with Him and through Him and in Him we too say, even unto death, *"Not my will!"* That is true Christian living. It was by the Eternal Spirit that Christ offered Himself to God without sin, especially in Gethsemane. That same Spirit lives and works in us. And in us, as in Christ, the keynote of the Spirit is Jesus' word of victory: *"not my will!"*

We must understand that without the Holy Spirit *"not my will"* looks like an unbearable burden. But God does not ask that we say it in our own strength. The joy of the Holy Spirit makes it possible and easy. Even as, with those words, the Son offered Himself to God a well-pleasing sacrifice, I may use the same words to place my life on the altar, a holy offering, well-pleasing to God. O Spirit of God, Spirit of Gethsemane and Golgotha, breathe on me and let my offering be *"not my will."*

Christian, let me ask you, This Christ, for whom *"not my will"* was life and joy, is He your Christ? Is He the Christ to whom you have offered your life so that He may make *"not my will"* your motto too? These words of Jesus glorified Him in the eyes of God; do they glorify Him in your eyes while He calls you and strengthens you to the same ideal? I beg of you, if you earnestly desire to experience the blessedness of God's love, let this Christ, the Christ of *"not my will,"* live in your heart. In things great and small, in your relationship to God and to your fellow men, may this ever be your love and your life: *"not my will"* — day after day, in Christ, by the power of the Holy Spirit.

Kneel before your precious Lord now and tell Him that by faith in His triumph in Gethsemane it will be so.

9

Lord, What Wilt Thou?

> And he [Saul] trembling and astonished said: Lord, *what wilt thou* have me to do? (Acts 9:6)

Many have asked what could be the secret of the amazing devotion and power in the life of Saul. The above words give us one answer. At the time of his conversion, as soon as he knew who it was that called him, *he surrendered himself to the will of the Lord.* "Lord! What wilt thou have me to do?" That shows us how his new life began, the root of it, the outstanding characteristic and the power of it. His life was so wonderful and fruitful because he remained true to those words. He lived *to do the will of his Lord.*

There are many lessons to be learned here.

The Lord has a will for each of us, His plan for our life, according to which He wants us to live.

He Himself wants to make His will known to each one.

He wants us to ask Him to reveal His will — His will for us all in general as well as for each one in particular.

Such a request, sincerely made, implies willingness to give oneself to His will and our lives in its service.

And we may be sure that He will answer such prayer. He will not require His child to do His will without making it clear to him. He will lead the child who wants to be led.

We may well ponder earnestly and pray about these words of Paul and still other implications of them. But my intention in this meditation is to concentrate your attention on one simple yet profound lesson that involves all the others and was mentioned at the beginning, *Christian conversion is nothing less than complete abandonment of one's will to do the will of God and of Christ.*

Do not say, "But of course; we know that." Most Christians do not know it. And it may be that you have never fully understood what this means: True conversion is such a complete yielding of my will that never again under any circumstances will I seek it, but I will always, with all the strength I have, seek only to know and do God's will.

Am I no longer to have a will of my own, then? Oh, yes! You need your will every day to do the great work for which God gave it to you — to accept and to will what He wills. The glory and the blessedness of a child of God is to be able to say: My will shall be merged with the heavenly, holy, perfect will of God. That is the highest possible expression of my will — to exert all its strength in the willing and doing of God's will. Think how wonderful, how great an honor, to be able to say that my will is the same as God's will! Like a certain saint of long ago, we can exult: "What a happy life I have! I always get my way, because God's will and mine always agree!"

Such a surrender of the will to God is not only conversion and the beginning of Christian life, it is also its growth and its strength. There is no better remedy for the complaints and ills in your life than this, that you resolve to do God's will in everything. Many a Christian sighs because of darkness and prays for light and joy, forgetting that there is only one way to attain these — the lovely and blessed will of God. God's will is nothing less than the revelation of His divine perfection. The sure and only way to find God is by doing His will. Remember this: By doing God's will you draw close to Him.

And if one should say he does not know God's will, or he has not the strength to do it, our text has the answer to that, too. Paul asks the Lord to make His will known. Knowledge of God's will obtained by prayer brings with it the power to do that will. What I learn merely with my mind from the law or from the Word does not give me life or power. But what the Spirit teaches me from the law or the Word by way of prayer gives life and strength. The Spirit enables me to see what is His will; He writes it on my heart; He also breathes into me the desire and the strength to do it.

Young Christian, do take to heart these two things as the rule of your life: *I may not and will not do anything else than the will of God.* It is for this I have been saved. And then expect, as any servant would expect from his master, that *the Lord will make His will clear to you in answer to prayer.* Make this your daily prayer: "Lord, I am ready to do Thy will; what dost Thou want me to do?" The Lord will surely answer you, and in such complete surrender to the will of God you will find the secret of an entirely new and joyful life.

10

Knowing God's Will

> And he [Ananias] said, The God of our fathers hath
> chosen thee, *that thou shouldest know his will,* and see that
> Just One (Acts 22:14).

Saul, on his way to Damascus, had prayed, "Lord,
what wilt thou have me to do?" In Damascus Ananias told
him that God had ordained him *to know His will* and to see
and hear the Lord Jesus. Besides the heavenly vision of
Jesus in His glory, there was this second blessing God had
prepared for him — that he would know God's will and
perform it. This is no less true of other Christians. God has
called you and me to see the Lord Jesus as exalted Savior
and Lord and to know His will.

Sad to say, many Christians separate these two. They
are happy and thankful to God for bringing them to where
they see the Righteous One and find salvation in Him. But
they are not equally happy, nor do they thank God, for
ordaining that they should know His will. They have not
grasped the wonderful truth that the glory of Christ lies in

this: He revealed and fulfilled the will of God when He came to redeem us; His perfection lies in perfect obedience to God's will; He always did the will of the Father; the salvation He wrought enables others to do His will; and the only way to experience the blessedness of salvation is to know and do that will.

To live a healthy Christian life, one must understand the great purpose of redemption. It is that I should know God's will in order to do it. God's will is the revelation of His eternal divine perfection. All beauty and splendor in the universe has been wrought by His will and radiates His will. The bliss of man before the Fall consisted of perfect harmony with God's will. He willed what God willed; his delight was God's delight. There is no delight for God or man except in God's holy and perfect will. Therefore the one supreme task of the Lord Jesus was to bring man, who had fallen outside the will of God, back into harmony with that will.

My motivation for the writing of this little book is the fact that I have found ignorance of this to be the cause of much weakness among Christians. I am deeply convinced that a change in this one particular would bring about a complete change in many lives. For this reason I would ask my readers a few questions, earnestly and simply. May God use them to bring you to genuine joy of salvation!

Have you understood and do you agree that the great work of salvation was wrought for the purpose of bringing about harmony of your will with God's?

Has this led you to so commit yourself to God that you want to seek your highest good and only blessedness in knowing and choosing and doing God's will, at any cost?

Do you consider it your highest privilege, an inestimable honor, that God should make His will known to you? And can you honestly say, "I want to know God's will in all things; there is only one thing in all the universe that I fear — failure to know and to do God's will"?

If you find you have not yet come to this insight, or

maybe you are frightened at the thought because you feel you do not have the strength to carry out such a resolution, I beg of you, do not withhold any longer from our God that which is His due — your entire will. Kneel before Him and say, "Father, I would know Thy will in all things; I want to live only to do the will of my God." Persist in such surrender and believe that God will accept it; He will give you the strength to carry it out. And do not rest until, by means of meditation and dedication and prayer, the word shall be imprinted upon your heart, as if spoken to you personally: *"God has ordained that you should know His will."*

What strength and stability and courage it gives one to know he is living only to do God's will! What an incentive to prayer! How it strengthens his trust! And what courage it gives in the struggle against sin to know: "I have been saved to do the will of God!"

11

He Who Does the Whole Will of God Is the Man After God's Own Heart

> I have found David the son of Jesse, a man after mine own heart, *which shall fulfill all my will* (Acts 13:22; cf. 1 Sam. 13:14).

How frequently we hear the comment about King David that he was a man after God's own heart. And how seldom we hear what follows: who shall fulfill all God's will. Yet these two are really inseparable. What was it that made David a man after God's heart? Simply this, that he would perform all the will of God. This differentiated him from Saul, who, for example in the matter of Amalek, performed only half of God's will, mingling his own will with God's, doing his own will under the pretense of obedience to God. Such behavior still differentiates the double-hearted Christian from the man of undivided commitment.

The one has never fully understood that he is called to give up his own will entirely to God's and must not do anything just "on his own"; the other desires to know only

God's will and to do it entirely. It is only the latter who is a man after God's heart.

Would you not wish that God would say about you, in contrast to what He says about the many who are like Saul, "I have found a man after my heart, who shall do all my will"? It is possible! Even though your station in life is nothing compared to David's, your gifts are few, and your place is among the humble and unknown, God needs a man after His heart just where you are, one willing to do all His will. Each of us has a particular calling, a place no one else can fill. God looks for a person to do all His will in each place. Do you want to be such a one? Or will you not at least try with all your heart to be one who answers to this twofold description of a friend of God: a man after God's heart, who will do all His will? God's heart is a deep mystery; His will is a revelation of that mystery. The man who seeks to do all of God's will is on the way to becoming a man after His heart.

A man after God's heart — who would not long to be such? Or are you only looking for God to help you and save you, without being concerned about whether or not you please Him? O Lord, make us ashamed of the self-seeking that looks only for our own salvation! Awaken in us a deep desire not merely to be saved but to be pleasing to Thee, a man after Thy heart. Jehu once asked Jehonadab, "Is thine heart right, as my heart is with thy heart?" And Jehonadab answered, "It is" (2 Kings 10:15). God asks the same of us. His heart is right with us. We are assured of this by His Word, by the giving of His Son, by His love. He asks if our heart is right with Him. May we be able to answer, "It is; yes, it is." My one desire is to have a heart that is right with God, even as God's heart is right with me, to be a man after His heart.

But is that really possible? Yes. In fact, this is what God has intended for us and wants to work within us. The first step toward that end is simple. Decide to be one of whom God can say, "I have found a man who shall do all My will." God is seeking such — people who are wholly committed to do His will. Offer yourself for such service and step out of the divided life into a life of undivided loyalty.

No doubt you have begun to feel that the weakness of your spiritual life has resulted from a lack of insight; you did not realize you were called *to do all God's will*. You never set yourself to that. You had not thought it possible, or that God required it. My brother, my sister, God does require it! And therefore He will also enable you to do it. Even as a father expects certain things of each of his children according to their age and ability, so the will of God requires of each of us according to the measure of grace He has given. But what He expects of you He will truly enable you to do.

I beg of you not to delay in making the good choice. Tell the Lord, in all humility, "Lord, until now I have never longed to be a person entirely after Thy heart. But from this time on that is what I want. Until now I had no real desire to do all Thy will. But now that is my desire. I shall never be content until Thy grace has made me one who is after Thy heart, willing to do all Thy will."

12

Being at Peace With God's Will

And when he [Paul] would not be persuaded, we
ceased, saying: *The will of the Lord be done* (Acts 21:14).

Paul was in Caesarea, on his way to Jerusalem. Agabus,
a prophet, declared through the Holy Spirit that Paul
would be taken captive by the Jews and turned over to the
Romans. His friends pleaded with him not to go on. But
Paul told them he was ready not only to be bound but even
to die for the name of the Lord Jesus. When his friends
realized they could not persuade him, they answered,
"The will of the Lord be done." They submitted to what
they saw to be God's will.

This story teaches us how we can find rest for our hearts
during the darkest hours and face whatever causes fear
and sorrow — *"The will of the Lord be done."*

There is a difference between *the will of God's good pleas-
ure,* the will that comes from the loving heart of a holy
God, and His *permissive will,* His will as Sovereign over all.
The first includes all that is right and good, which He

therefore approves and commands. The second covers everything that happens, even the activities of the wicked. Nothing occurs in the whole universe apart from His permissive will. It was not the will of God's good pleasure that Paul should be delivered to his enemies, but it was His permissive will.

It is one of the greatest comforts in the life of a Christian to grasp this truth: Whatever unpleasant event may come to him comes with God's permission, and therefore the problems and difficulties in which he finds himself are God's will for him. It is not God's will that someone should hate or persecute me; God does not will sin. But if someone should hate me or persecute me I know that God has permitted it and that the trials and the suffering are His will for me.

Once I have accepted this, I can turn my attention away from the cause of my difficulty and from the people who bother me and fix my heart on God who has willed that I endure this suffering. Then I can begin to follow the example of Jesus, who accepted the betrayal of a Judas and the hatred of a Caiaphas as God's will, as a cup the Father had given Him to drink. Then no power on earth or in hell can rob me of my peace of heart, the assurance that God's will has brought me into this situation.

In order that you may always enjoy this blessing, let me teach you four simple lessons:

1. When you are tried or afflicted, remind yourself immediately: *I am here by God's will, exactly where He planned I should be.* Whether the trial came because of the hatred of an enemy or the disloyalty of a friend, through fault of my own or by the direct guidance of God, my being in this difficulty is His will. To that will I submit myself; that is my first concern. Being in His will, I find peace. In fact, at this moment I could not be in better circumstances because right here I am within His will. The will of the Lord be done!

2. Then you may also confidently and boldly say, *"God, having brought me into this difficulty, will surely give me the grace*

to conduct myself in it as I ought." Quiet submission, unwavering trust, and complete surrender to His will, by which I must honor Him, these He Himself will work within me. I dare to expect this, without a doubt; He brought me here and He is also watching over me here.

3. You may go even farther and say, *"God Himself will teach me why He brought me into this trial."* It is for our sanctification that He chastises us, to deliver us from the power of the flesh and the world, from self-will and the desire to please self, to humble us and make us childlike and heavenly minded. Therefore, I can be sure He who placed me in this crucible is watching the process most carefully, the purifying and perfecting. Knowing this, I give myself wholeheartedly to His will, saying, "Let Him do what is right in His own eyes. The will of the Lord be done!"

4. Then you will also dare to say, *"God's will, which brought me here, can also bring me out of my troubles, at His own time and in His own way."* His work is to carry out the plan that, in His love, He designed for me; my part is to surrender myself wholly to His will. That is what I want to do. Whether with tears or with joy, in quiet submission or with good cheer, I would always live as the citizens of heaven live, with one desire in my heart: *The will of the Lord be done!*

What a blessing it is to know that the darkest trials, the most bitter distresses, as well as the smallest disappointments and the quickly passing fears, can all work together to make my will more completely one with the glorious will of my God.

13

Knowing and Not Doing God's Will

> Behold, thou art called a Jew . . . and makest thy boast
> of God, and *knowest his will* . . . and art confident that thou
> thyself art . . . an instructor of the foolish. . . . Thou
> therefore which teachest another, teachest thou not thy-
> self? thou that preachest a man should not steal, dost thou
> steal? (Rom. 2:17-21).

You recall how solemnly Jesus warned us that not those
who say "Lord! Lord!" but only those who *do the Father's
will* shall enter the kingdom of heaven (Matt. 7:21). Here
Paul utters the same warning. He tells the Jew, who boasts
that he knows God's will and puts his trust in that knowledge, that knowing God's will profits him nothing unless
he also does it. In the days of our Lord, such boasting was
characteristic of those who were students of the Scrip-
tures. They were proud of their knowledge of the Word.
This is also one of the great dangers of regular Bible
reading and church attendance: we enjoy gaining new and
clearer insights into God's truths and even feel blessed in

doing so, though meanwhile we may be making little progress in the doing of His will. We enjoy *knowing* God's will more than *doing* it. Our religion is then of the head rather than of the heart. That is a dreadful danger.

There is no way to avoid this except to keep in the forefront of our mind as we read God's Word that His only reason for making His will known is that we should do it, and that whatever He reveals of His will I want to do. Merely knowing His will can only bring me grief, deceiving me with an appearance of piety, or hardening me in disobedience if I fail to do it. God makes His will known with the expectation that I do it. Doing His will is the only way to please Him and become receptive for His holiness and His love.

The only reason I want to know God's will is that I may do it. If that is your sincere desire, it might be well to write the following on the flyleaf of your Bible: "Even as I want to believe with all my heart every promise of God found in this Book, *I want also, with all my heart, to carry out every command of God found in this Book.*"

Read it every time you use your Bible and think of it every time you hear the Word preached. Be alert to catch the indications of His will and learn to say humbly, "I have discovered something God wants me to do, and I will go right out to do it." Do not read too much at a time; rather, ponder every revelation of God's will and let it penetrate deeply into your heart. In the first Psalm we read, *"Blessed is the man whose delight is in the law of the Lord; and in His law doth he meditate day and night."* Meditate on each command with joy and love until its rich meaning and beauty expand before your eyes. And then, above all, pray that God's Spirit will implant His will in your heart.

The reason we lack the strength to do God's will, even thinking perhaps that we cannot or do not have to do it, is that we consent to it only with our human understanding. That makes it a dead letter. It is the Spirit that gives life. "The words I speak unto you, they are spirit and they are life" (John 6:63). The Holy Spirit must reveal God's words to our hearts; He must make them spirit and life. The law cannot make alive; the commandment leads to death as long as we try to grasp it with human understanding and obey it in our own strength.

Set yourself quietly in the presence of God; let the Holy Spirit work in your heart; commit yourself completely to the will of God; pray humbly that the Spirit within you may make the words you read spirit and life. He will do so. Such knowledge of God's will becomes living knowledge, which satisfies the longings and the love of the heart, truly unites the will to God's will, and thus gives the desire and the strength to do it.

You are a Christian. You glory in God; you know His will; but are you *doing* it? That is the question. Do make up your mind no longer to permit such a discrepancy between your *knowledge* and your *walk,* no longer to allow your *knowing* to be so far ahead of your *doing.* The Holy Spirit can make the two go hand in hand. What He teaches you to see He also teaches you to do. He is one Spirit — the Spirit of light and of power. If you know God's will only with the mind, you cannot do it; if the Holy Spirit teaches you, He also gives power to carry it out. Then you will experience the blessing of Psalm 1: "Blessed is the man . . . [whose] delight is in the law of the Lord; and in his law doth he meditate day and night. *And he shall be like a tree planted by the rivers of water, that bringeth forth his fruit in his season; his leaf also shall not wither; and whatsoever he doeth shall prosper."*

14

Renewing of the Mind Necessary to Prove God's Will

And be not conformed to this world; but be ye transformed by the renewing of your mind, that ye may prove what is that *good, and acceptable, and perfect, will of God* (Rom. 12:2).

The practical portion of Paul's letter to the Romans begins with the first verse of chapter 12. There, as you know, Paul pleads with believers to present their bodies as an acceptable offering to God. Give yourselves completely to God; live as people wholly devoted to God. In verse 2 Paul continues his plea, urging those who have thus dedicated themselves to God to prove — that is, to find out and make sure — what the good and acceptable and perfect will of God is, if they would live a life pleasing to Him. Anyone who truly desires to be *a sacrifice well-pleasing to God* must live *a life well-pleasing to Him.* And we are well-pleasing to Him only if we live within His will.

Good, acceptable, and perfect — these three expressions mean, first of all, that if I want to make sure of the will of God in my daily life, I must distinguish between good and evil and recognize the good as God's will; then I must find out exactly what His will is for me — what is acceptable and well-pleasing to Him. Thus I will come to know the perfect will of God, the totality of all He asks of me.

In order to know and to do what is well-pleasing to God, two things are mentioned as indispensable. One is *"Be not conformed to this world."* Such conformity is your greatest danger, and you must be on the watch for it. The second is *"Be transformed by the renewing of your mind."* This you will find to be the only source of your strength. He who heeds both the warning and the admonition will surely know and do the will of God.

Listen carefully to the warning: *"Be not conformed to this world."* "The friendship of the world is enmity with God" (James 4:4). The world seeks to please self, not God. The world hated and rejected the Son of God. He was not of this world, neither is His kingdom. By nature we are of the world. After we have been reborn, we are still in the world and still very much influenced by it. Its impact on our thoughts and our behavior is strong and continuous, though we may not even be aware of it. Unless we are deeply in earnest about withdrawing and separating ourselves from its pleasures and its standards, striving not to conform in any way, living as "not of the world," we shall not be sensitive to the will of God. Spiritual matters, and especially the will of God, can only be discerned spiritually. "We have received, not the spirit of the world, but the spirit which is of God; that we might know the things that are freely given to us of God" (1 Cor. 2:12). Remember this: a worldly mind, even of a Christian, cannot know the will of God.

The warning is followed by admonition: *"But be ye transformed by the renewing of your mind."* God's Word speaks not only of a once-for-all regeneration as the beginning of spiritual life, but also of a continued renewal by the Spirit. "Be renewed in the spirit of your mind." "He has saved us

49

by the washing of regeneration, and renewing of the Holy Ghost" (Titus 3:5).

The life of the Holy Spirit is His continuous, uninterrupted, living work within us. Hence the admonition: "Be renewed in the spirit of your mind" (Eph. 4:23). Be changed each day from what you formerly were, and from the world around you, in the spirit of your mind, by the Spirit of God who dwells in you. Only then — and most surely then — will you be able to discern the will of God.

Here is a lesson of great importance. Sometimes we are ignorant of the will of God; sometimes the little we think we know about it has little effect upon our lives; too often we know His will but do not get around to doing it. And the reason is simply this: *The spirit of the world is too much with us.* We make no real effort to understand and heed the warning: "Be not conformed to this world." The will of God belongs to heavenly things, and only the mind that longs to partake of the heavenly and is willing to be changed and renewed day after day by the Spirit of God can understand it.

Christian, do you long to be a person after God's own heart — one who wills to do all His will? Then hear what He says: "Be not conformed to this world, but be ye transformed by the renewing of your mind." The Spirit of the Son, whom the Father has sent to live in your heart, is at work within you. Trust in Him. Submit yourself to His guidance. The renewing of your mind is His work. As you are changed by the power of His indwelling, you learn to know the will of God and have strength to do it.

O my God, in Christ Jesus I have laid myself upon Thy altar, a living and holy sacrifice, well-pleasing unto Thee. As one dedicated to God, one who longs to be "after Thy heart," I do not want to be at all conformed to this world. I would surrender myself to be changed by the Spirit, that in everything I may *know Thy will* — that it is good and well-pleasing to Thee, and perfect — and that my life may be wholly devoted to doing Thy will.

15

It Is God's Will That Christ Should Draw Us Out of the World

> Who gave himself for our sins, that he might deliver us
> from this present evil world, *according to the will of God and
> our Father* (Gal. 1:4).

In our previous meditations we saw how *the world* and
the will of God are opposed to each other. One who is
conformed to the world must be changed by the renewing
of his mind before he can *know the will of God*. Today we
will consider the same problem from a different angle —
when Christ gave Himself for our sins, it was *to deliver us
from the world, according to the will of God*. The will of God and
the world are two powers arrayed against each other, in
conflict with each other. Both exert on our minds an
influence that we are hardly aware of but that is very
powerful. It is important for a Christian who would know
the will of God to be alert to this and learn how to conduct
himself toward the world. He must know that it is God's
will that he be totally delivered from it, so that though he
is still in the world, he is not at all of the world. He must

also know that God wills him to be drawn out of it by Christ.

The *world* — that word includes every relationship of fallen man to things around him. God created the world good, but when man listened to the serpent and chose the pleasure of the visible things in preference to obedience to God, he and the world with him fell into the power of Satan. And the world, which should have served him by pointing him to God, became his master and a deceiver, keeping him from God. Jesus came as one "not of this world" and says of His disciples, "They are not of this world, even as I am not of this world" (John 17:16). He came to draw us from the present wicked world. And the young Christian must understand that this is the work Christ wants to do — draw him out of "this present evil world," because that is God's will. He must see that this is God's will and must heartily cooperate.

When a Christian has come to know that this is God's will and heartily consents to it, he must learn how it can be done. Christ does it within us. He gave Himself for our sins to draw us out of the world. Sin, by way of the law, gave the world and Satan legal power over us. But Christ gave Himself for sin, to make reconciliation and to conquer it. By granting us full pardon, He rescues us completely from the power of sin. And now, as the living and exalted Victor over sin, it is His task to draw us out of the world and deliver us from its influence.

How does He do this? Happy is the one who knows and understands the answer: He does it *by His personal attractiveness*. The deceptive attractiveness of the world appeals to us, wins our hearts, and draws us away from God. But the heavenly winsomeness of Jesus' person, winning the love of our hearts, draws us away from the world. Let us not, however, think of this as an attraction to one who is above us and outside of us. No, it is Christ in our hearts, actually living there, embraced and held close by our love, becoming more and more precious to us, satisfying our every desire. Thus He draws us from the evil world.

And how can I come to experience this wonderful work of His grace? Certainly not by taking a position halfway between Christ and the world and asking the Lord to draw me back every time I go too far. Oh no! Christ and the world are opposed to each other; I must renounce the world entirely, even though I am not yet entirely freed from its influence. I must choose for Christ without reservation, consenting wholeheartedly to God's will, to His plan for delivering me from this evil world. I must fix my heart, all my affections, on Christ. And He, like a heavenly magnet, will draw me away from all the attractions of the world and from the spirit of the world.

Dear reader, you see now that the will of God does not consist of a series of laws. It goes far deeper and far higher. It includes the whole wonderful plan He has for our sanctification and glorification. The better you see this, the more eager you will be to surrender yourself to it. It is Christ, who came to do the will of God, who brings this to pass and fulfills it in you gloriously. "Lo, I come . . . to do thy will, O God" (Heb. 10:7). There is a depth of meaning in those words of Jesus; He came only to do God's will on earth; He also moves me to do God's will as I learn to know Him and love Him. It is He who draws me away from the world when I have personal fellowship with Him. The more He becomes my "all in all," the more the will of God will be fulfilled in me and the more I will be wholly freed from the world.

16

Pray to Be Filled With the Knowledge of God's Will

> For this cause we . . . do not cease to pray for you . . . that
> ye might be *filled with the knowledge of his will* in all wisdom
> and spiritual understanding (Col. 1:9).

The Colossians were young Christians, recently come out of heathen darkness into the light. They were in need of many things. One for which Paul prayed most earnestly was this: that they might know God's will and be filled with such knowledge, in all wisdom and spiritual understanding.

To grasp the importance of this prayer and realize that *to know God's will* is at the root of a strong Christian life, note what Paul says about the result of the answer to such a prayer, the blessing that comes to the heart filled with the knowledge of God's will. He says, "That ye might be filled with the knowledge of His will in *all* wisdom and spiritual understanding; that ye might walk worthy of the Lord unto *all* pleasing" (Col. 1:9,10). He who is *filled* with the knowledge of His will in *all* wisdom will walk worthy of the Lord and be pleasing to Him in *all* things. Also, he will be fruitful in *all* good works. Even more, he will be strengthened with *all* might, even "unto *all* patience and longsuffering, with joyfulness; giving thanks unto the Father . . ." (Col. 1:11,12).

Did you notice — *all, all,* and again, *all*? There must be nothing niggardly or stingy in the Christian's life. A Christian's walk should be pleasing in all respects, with all good works, strengthened with all power, filled with all patience and longsuffering. And that cannot be unless it is first of all filled with the knowledge of God's will, in all wisdom and spiritual understanding.

Take your Bible and reread this great prayer of Paul; I feel sure you will be convinced that to be filled with the knowledge of the will of God in all wisdom is the one thing above all that every young Christian needs. He must not be content with the little that he knows of God's will. He may not suppose he knows enough already, more even than he can carry out. The more he knows of that will and longs to be filled with the knowledge of it in *all* wisdom, the more he will be strengthened with *all* power.

And how can one be thus filled with the knowledge of God's will, in all wisdom and spiritual power? The answer is simple. Paul prays for it. He says, I "do not cease to pray for you and to desire that you may be filled." You must make it your specific desire. Remember — you cannot know God, or love Him, or please Him, or enjoy Him except by loving and doing His will. Remember that you were saved to do His will. Remember that doing His will is the glory of heaven and the blessedness of life here below. Above all, do remember that your likeness to the Lord Jesus lies in your will being one with His. To be filled with the knowledge of His will — that is something to be desired more than the daily food for your body. Pray for it, specifically, persistently, without ceasing. Tell God that you will not cease to pray for it. Your prayer will be answered.

And do not forget these words: *"in all wisdom and spiritual*

55

understanding." Spiritual understanding and wisdom are attained only by the guidance of the Holy Spirit. And the guidance of the Spirit is not a matter of the head but of the heart. God has sent the Spirit of His Son into your heart. Know that He is there; honor Him; be afraid to do anything that might grieve Him; give yourself wholly to follow His guidance. Let your will be wholly surrendered to the will of God. Determine not to cease praying to be filled with the knowledge of His will. The Holy Spirit will surely satisfy the hungry heart and grant all wisdom and spiritual understanding.

Christian, your great need is to know and to do God's will. Pray earnestly that your heart may be filled with that will; then it will become evident also in your life.

17

About the Spiritual Understanding
of God's Will

> Wherefore be ye not unwise, but understanding what
> the will of the Lord is (Eph. 5:17).

The Bible speaks of two kinds of understanding. There
is the merely human understanding, the "fleshly mind"
(Col. 2:18), which may know much about the Bible and
speak freely about it but does not know the power of it.
The other is the "spiritual understanding" (Col. 1:9),
whereby the heart is actually filled with the knowledge of
God's will so that it lives within him. We know that the
Holy Spirit has been given to be our teacher, to lead us
into the truth; if He lives and rules in our hearts, He gives
us a spiritual understanding of God's will. The words of
our text — "understanding what the will of the Lord is"
— are immediately followed by these: "and be filled with
the Spirit." By changing the spirit of our mind, a work
progressively accomplished by the Holy Spirit, we come
to know and understand God's will.

"Understanding what the will of the Lord is." If that is

our desire, we must not have the notion that God's will is identical with His laws and commandments. The will of God is a much broader concept. First of all, it means *the council or the intention of His eternal good pleasure,* according to which He is working out all of history (see Eph. 1:5,9,11). This includes choosing us to be children of God through Jesus Christ *"according to the good pleasure of His will"* and gathering together into one all things in Christ, a revealed mystery *of His will.* He is the one who "worketh all things after the counsel of his own will." Whatever He wills shall happen. Creation, redemption, the blessings and joys of His creatures, the enmity against whatever is sinful — all these are included in God's *good pleasure,* His holy and loving will.

Then there is also *the will of God in His providence,* which controls the whole universe, even permits sin and allows the temptations and resulting miseries that come upon humankind.

A Christian must learn to look on all that happens on earth in this light that God gives us: everything, including the suffering that may be his portion, no matter what its source, is included in the will of God.

There is also *the will of God in His commandments,* found in the precepts of the Word of God. These give us the broad principles according to which we should live. Application of these to particular circumstances must be made known to us by the guidance of the Holy Spirit. The Word tells me that I must take time to pray and I must give money to the poor, but in neither does it say how much. The Spirit of God will direct each of us individually in such matters.

Finally, there is also *the will of God in His promises.* If I would obey the injunction "Understand what the will of the Lord is," I must realize that God's will for me is found not only in what He prohibits but also in what He promises. When I grasp this, that every promise of God is a revelation of His will for me, I discover that I do not merely have a right to these things; I am also obligated to

58

open the way for them. It is not a matter of choice. I am called to give myself wholly to the will of God, to His plan for me, also as expressed in His promises.

"Understanding what the will of the Lord is." His will envelops the whole universe, controls all that is and everything that happens; by prayer we learn what He wants us to do, and in His promises we learn what He will do. It is all one and the same will. How we need spiritual understanding to grasp it all — His eternal good pleasure, His divine permissiveness in time, His holy commandments, and His glorious promises!

One thing in particular is very necessary if we would understand the heavenly will of God: complete surrender to that will. Think of it as the revelation of God's life-giving power and of His love; you cannot know these apart from His will. You must yield yourself freely and gladly to this will as the loving power that upholds the universe and will uphold you. Do not begin with burdensome things, things that are hard to understand, or to carry out, or to bear. Rather, begin by thinking of God's will in the light of His love and His greatness, accepting it as including all things, and losing yourself in it. With strong determination, set your heart to do God's will whenever you can discern what it is. Put yourself in the center of His will, allowing it to possess you and control you. Then you shall have the courage and the will to bear whatever it may bring, to obey its every injunction, and to open your heart to every promise. It will become a joy to you. Only those who live in the center of His will can rightly understand it.

18

Do God's Will From the Heart

> Servants, be obedient to them that are your masters
> according to the flesh, with fear and trembling, in single-
> ness of your heart, *as unto Christ,* not with eyeservice, as
> men-pleasers, but as the servants *of Christ, doing the will of
> God from the heart;* with good will doing service, as to the
> Lord and not to men (Eph. 6:5-7).

In the early days of Christianity slavery was common.
All servants were slaves. And in those days the church was
composed largely of the lowly and despised, many of them
slaves. That is why we find many and long admonitions
addressed to slaves. These admonitions are full of meaning for us because they show us that faith in Christ enables
us to serve the Lord in even the most difficult positions and
circumstances. They present the underlying principles by
which one who is oppressed or even abused can neverthe-
less do his work with joy and experience the blessedness of
knowing that the Lord looks upon it as a pleasing sacrifice
that He will reward. A slave's work can be as much a
heavenly service as the work of an angel.

Just what are the principles that glorify the work of slaves and enable a slave to do his work with joy? We find the first one in the words "be obedient to . . . your masters . . . , *doing the will of God from the heart.*" The slave had to accept his position as slave, and with it the work and the suffering, as *God's will.* Accepting the hard work as the will of God could sweeten it, take the sting out of it for him. He could find courage and even heavenly joy in this confidence: In doing my work I am doing God's will; the humblest task has heavenly meaning and worth; I am busy doing what He wants me to do.

Sad to say, many Christians have never learned to see the will of their heavenly Father in their earthly lot. Therefore they never experience the heart-warming joy of being able to say concerning their humble tasks: "The angels are doing the will of God, and so am I! The will of God is revealed to me not only in the commandments of Scripture, but also in His providence, which led me into this place and laid certain obligations upon me. I must acknowledge His guidance and try to do the work assigned to me as *the will of God* and do it *from the heart.* Yes, from the heart — with inner contentment and even joy, because my Father's will is always love and blessing." Thus our eyes are closed to what men see and opened to what God sees. *Doing the will of God from the heart* — that makes all the difference in life, floods it with God's light.

But how can one really come to that point? For this, the text presents a second principle. Note how it points the slave to his Savior three times: Be obedient to your masters *as unto Christ;* not as men-pleasers but as the *servants of Christ;* with good will doing service as *to the Lord* and not to men. The apostle reckoned that, through the Holy Spirit, the Lord Jesus was so near to these people, dwelling within them, and their hearts could be so joyful in His love, that they would no longer think of the severity of their master or the difficulty of their work. A mere thought of Jesus, or of the forgiveness of their sins, was not enough to make them willing to endure slavery as the will of God and to obey a hard master as they would obey Christ. More than that was required. *The actual presence of Christ,* who was more real to them than their owner, His love and joy in their hearts — these could enable them to accept all their burden of slavery, as servants of Christ, with "good will."

Shall we not ask our Lord to grant us His constant nearness in such measure that we may be assured of His presence in all things and at all times? Then it will be easy to do all our work as unto the Lord. Even in our day there are servants who have professed that a great change came into their lives when they experienced the indwelling presence of the Lord. Whatever their work, they could then do it with joy, singing as they served the Lord, doing His will from the heart no matter how humble or distasteful the task. If we take courage and truly believe that even as an earthly master keeps an eye on his slaves and their work, so our Lord is ever near us, watching over us in love, then we certainly need not hesitate to give ourselves to do His will heartily, in everything. And he who does so, trusting in the exalted Lord, may be sure that He will grant His presence, demonstrating it by giving His strength.

19

Stand Perfect and Complete in the Will of God

> Epaphras . . . a servant of Christ, saluteth you, always laboring fervently for you in prayers,. that ye may *stand perfect and complete in all the will of God* (Col. 4:12).

In Colossians 1 Paul prayed that they might be *filled with the knowledge of the will of God,* in order to walk worthy of the Lord *"unto all pleasing."* Here in chapter 4 Epaphras prays for them, asking much the same, also referring them to the will of God. He "labors fervently" in prayer that they may — note well — *"stand perfect and complete in all the will of God."*

In his prayer, as in Paul's, the chief concern is the believer's attitude toward the will of God. We notice immediately the little word *all* in both prayers, reminding us that there should be no divided loyalty. Paul asked, you recall, that they "might be filled with the knowledge of His will in *all* wisdom and spiritual understanding . . . unto *all* pleasing, being fruitful in *every* good work . . . with *all* might . . . unto *all* patience." Epaphras asks that they may stand perfect and complete in *all* the will of God. *In all the will of God*, nothing excepted! *"Stand"* suggests firmness, not merely seeking His will but standing, like a tree firmly rooted in the ground, *"perfect and complete."* Not fearful, lest it be too great or too high. Epaphras prays for nothing less than a complete commitment to all of God's will.

For this he "labors" in prayer. The word used is a strong expression indicating a struggle. It is the same word used to describe the Lord's prayers in Gethsemane. Prayer was no simple, easy matter for Him. He knew that there are forces that oppose all who pray, forces that must be overcome by persistent and fervent prayer before God will answer. He knew too that all of Satan's power is concentrated against the will of God. This was the point at which Christ's struggle in Gethsemane triumphed over the power of darkness. A similar struggle will be required of us if we would reach the goal of standing perfect and complete in the will of God. Be prepared, dear Christian, to take up the struggle, to labor in prayer, if you would have this blessing. May it be your sincere desire to *stand perfect and complete in the will of God*.

To that end consider the following suggestions: First of all, commit yourself to the will of God in its widest outreach. Ponder the great truth that nothing is more perfect, more beautiful, more lovely, more blessed and powerful. Cultivate the conviction that there is nothing in all the world better or more wonderful for any one of us than to be in complete accord with God's will. Meditate and pray until your mind and heart are filled with the wonder of His will. Gradually the desire to be in full accord with that divine will must inevitably grow, till you find yourself saying again and again: *To live within His will, that is what I want*. Thus, commitment to God's will becomes a joyous act of faith, in the assurance that God will bring it to completion. Take a firm stand: I am one who is fully committed to the will of God.

Having made this beginning, you will discover that the glory of God's will gives heavenly light on particular circumstances from hour to hour, showing you details of that will. Whether His will is shown in disappointment or suffering that comes by way of His providence, or in a command that must be obeyed, perhaps with self-denial, or whether His will is revealed in His promises that are fulfilled as you walk in faith — give yourself to it continuously, without fear or reservation. Be prepared to bear, to do, to believe whatever may be His will.

If you persevere in giving yourself in this way, you will inevitably be driven to prayer. The struggle to "stand perfect in all the will of God" makes you aware of how little you know and how insufficient your own strength is. You discover you cannot carry out the will of God except by the strength of God Himself within you. You begin to see the will of God as the power that upholds the whole universe, the flowing fountain from which comes only what is holy and blessed, the source of all the spiritual gifts that God in lovingkindness bestows on you. Prayer becomes the natural expression of dependence, of continuous desire and surrender — an unceasing struggle against self-will and unbelief so that the will of God may have complete dominion over you. You will also learn by experience that the fervent prayer of a righteous man, of one who longs to stand perfect in the will of God, "availeth much."

20

Our Sanctification, the Will of God

For *this is the will of God*, even your sanctification (1 Thess. 4:3).

The few laws that Scripture contains are rays of light revealing only small portions of the whole of God's will, much as the words I write are parts of the thought I wish to express. He who would know the complete will of God must look for the larger concept, discover the real objectives. One main objective is given us in the above text: "This is the will of God, even your sanctification."

Sanctified — made holy. God alone is the Holy One. There is none other who is holy in himself. There is no holiness apart from Him and where there is holiness He has bestowed it. Nor can He give His holiness except by giving Himself. Holiness is an attribute of God, a part of His being, inseparable from His very existence. We have only as much of holiness as we have of God. Therefore He says, "I am the Lord that doth sanctify you" (Exod. 31:13). God the Father, the Holy One, sanctifies us. Of the

Son it is said that He is made unto us sanctification. The Spirit is called the Holy Spirit or the Spirit of sanctification. Our sanctification is the life and the work of the triune God within us.

"This is the will of God, even your sanctification" tells us that the whole of God's will in regard to our creation and redemption, in His precepts and His promises, aims only to make us holy as He is holy, that we may share His holy and blessed life. If we would experience the power of those words of Paul, we must take time to ponder them and to pray, allowing them to fill our hearts. This is the glorious, unchangeable, almighty will of God — that I shall be holy!

This will of God is so far beyond our usual thoughts that we simply cannot understand it unless the Spirit enlightens us. The eternal God desires my sanctification! We need to ask God to fill our minds with the power of this great truth, by the Holy Spirit.

The light of God and His power always go hand in hand. If I try to understand the will of God with my limited and darkened mind, I have only my limited and feeble strength with which to do it. But when I wait upon God so that through the Holy Spirit His will shines within me like a heavenly light and I am "filled with all knowledge and spiritual understanding," the Spirit will with the light also give power. Note well, the most complete knowledge of God's will, if it is acquired only by the natural mind, fails to give me the strength to perform it. On the other hand, every revelation concerning God's will that comes to me through the Holy Spirit strengthens me with heavenly power. So I must fervently pray, "Lord, help me understand how earnestly God wills my sanctification!"

This great truth, when we are led by the Spirit to see it, inspires amazing courage. God wants me to be holy; it is His heart's desire; therefore, I may be sure that He will work it within me. Believing this, we also see new meaning in the words "Christ is our sanctification." Holiness is no longer a hopeless struggle against innumerable sins, but an entering into the will of God, which was fulfilled by Christ and which the Spirit now works within us. Holiness, like God's will, is a revelation of God's love and power, and all that is required is complete surrender to it that He may complete His work in us. Each one of His commandments, as an expression of His will, is merely a small part of the great truth that the almighty God wills that we shall be holy even as He is holy.

Dear reader, do you not already feel a growing of your desire to lose yourself in His will? Do so, and He who works all things according to the counsel of His will will sanctify you. Try to keep these two thoughts together in your mind: God's precepts, even the least of them, I want to do, with all my heart, and His promises, even the greatest of them, I will believe with all my heart. Precept and promise are joined in the eternal will of God's holy love, to bring us to share His own perfection and joy. *"This is the will of God, even your sanctification."*

21

Always Giving Thanks, the Will of God

> In every thing give thanks: for this is *the will of God* in
> Christ Jesus concerning you (1 Thess. 5:18).

Giving thanks in everything is continuous joy. When someone receives what he has asked for, he is glad, and giving
thanks is the expression of his joy. God, like any father,
wants His children to be happy; He does not want to hear
complaint, or worry, or sighing. That is why His Word
tells us, Thank God in everything, for this is the will of
God for you.

Giving thanks in everything draws the mind away from self
and from the earth and lifts the soul upward to God. Our
prayers, our faith, and our love rise heavenward as if on
wings when we give thanks. God wants His children to
have a foretaste of heaven, where all is thanksgiving and
praise. Therefore, thank God in everything, for this is the
will of God for you.

Giving thanks in everything — there is always good reason
to do so. The child of God, if he has eyes, finds more

reason for thanksgiving than for complaint, even in the severest trial. We always have God! There is always His love for which to praise Him. If you can find nothing else for which to be thankful, you can still thank Him, in the midst of problems, that He still lives and still loves. Be a cheerful Christian. Show that you find pleasure in Him and that He is the source of your joy. Yes, thank God in everything, for this is His will for you.

Giving thanks in everything is what God Himself wants to work in you. What is impossible with men is possible with God. Many simply conclude that it cannot be done and shove aside the suggestion; they have no ears for this as the actual literal will of God. They may say they accept the will of God, but when it comes to this particular bit of God's will, they refuse to bow. Christian, do lay hold of this truth: It is the good, well-pleasing, and perfect will of God that I shall give thanks in everything. And decide: I must live accordingly; I want to and I will.

Giving thanks in everything — Christ works it in us. Read the words once more: "This is the will of God *in Christ Jesus* concerning you. There lies the secret. God's will is no longer a law given from Mount Sinai, which has neither life nor power. God's will *in Christ Jesus* is a life that He gives you, power to be free from the world, and which can fill you with heavenly joy. That you should always give thanks is part of the deliverance Jesus wrought. Live in Him. Abide in Him. And the songs of thanksgiving will flow spontaneously.

Giving thanks in everything is one of the fruits of "joy in the Holy Spirit" that is a characteristic of the kingdom of God (Rom. 14:17). I cannot be too insistent in warning you not to try to do the will of God, or expect to abide in Christ, or think you can give thanks in everything, without the indwelling and guidance of the Holy Spirit. The Holy Spirit was sent *from heaven* to fit us for life in heaven. How foolish it is, then, to attempt to live a heavenly life without knowing the joy of the Spirit's indwelling. Let each command of God that seems too exalted, and indeed every

70

part of His glorious perfect will, remind you of your inheritance as a child of God, *your only source of strength* to live as a child of God. As a child of God, you have the Spirit of God's Son in your heart, the gift of God. In His strength thank God in everything.

Giving thanks in everything gives us courage for work and makes us a blessing for the church and the world. Nothing is more appealing than cheerfulness. Men and animals were created to be happy. The joyful Christian — I do not mean a joyful person who happens also to be a Christian, but a Christian who joyfully does the will of God and is always thankful to God, under all circumstances — is the best possible recommendation for the gospel. Many have the idea that serving God means hardship, a life of unnatural self-denial. The Lord needs people as His witnesses who can demonstrate, by always being cheerful, that there is joy in self-denial — a self-denial in which, because they have forsaken all else, they glory and rejoice in the Lord.

Give thanks in everything. Do you now understand the wonder of it, how blessed it is that God wills this for you in Christ Jesus? Then begin at once. Begin this moment by thanking God that it is His will for you to be always thankful. Thank Him that He, as God, is the one glorious and inexhaustible reason for thanksgiving. Thank Him for revealing His will to you. And, through the Holy Spirit, begin a life in Christ in which there will never be an end to the giving of thanks, either on earth or in heaven.

22

The Salvation of All Men, the Will of God

> I exhort therefore, that, first of all, supplications, prayers, *intercessions . . . be made for all men.* . . . For this is good and acceptable in the sight of God our Saviour, who will have all men to be saved . . . (1 Tim. 2:1-4).
>
> The Lord is . . . longsuffering to us-ward, *not willing* that *any* should perish, but that *all* should come to repentance (2 Peter 3:9).

We have mentioned several times that those who would know and do the will of God must not merely think of certain commandments but must consider the broader revelation of God's will concerning man and what attitude and effort this requires. Nor should we limit ourselves to concern about His will for our individual lives, but rather learn His will for all men and use this as guideline for our behavior and feelings toward them. Reread the above two texts and note what we are taught — He wills "all men to be saved." He wills "that all should come to repentance." What effect should this will of God have on us? And how must we be united with His will?

Perhaps you will ask, "But how can I harmonize this with faith in the omnipotence of God, when it is evident that He does not grant repentance to all? Or how can I square it with what the Scripture teaches about election?" There is only one answer: It is not necessary for you to square these things or understand them. God is greater than your mind and heart. Accept what His Word teaches; believe in His love; and leave it to God to some day justify Himself. Your task is to prayerfully accept God's will and to receive it into your heart. Believe what is written: *God wills* that all men be saved, that all come to repentance. Let faith in those beautiful words take possession of your heart; allow God's will to become your will and inspire your life; perhaps then you will attain to some little understanding of how to harmonize this will of His with His omnipotence and His sovereignty.

If we accept this will of God, taking it into our hearts and making it truly ours, how will our lives be affected? The first result will be just what Paul commands — prayers and intercession *for all men.* We will learn to see each man in the proper light, not the light of who he is, what he does, or what he deserves, but in the light of God's love and God's will for him. If God so loved miserable and unworthy creatures and so desired to help them that He sent His Son to die for them, and if our will is one with His, we will be inspired to love them and pray earnestly for them. True love always expresses itself in deeds. Sincere prayer leads us to do what we can to obtain what we ask. If God's will that all people should be saved becomes our will, it is impossible not to do all we can to bring them to repentance.

This active response must reach out to all, far and near. Everyone has unconverted people living nearby. If God's will for their salvation really becomes our will, we are driven to offer ourselves to God to be used as messengers of the gospel of peace to them. The call to bring the gospel to all comes to every one of us. Whoever is convinced of God's will concerning the heathen becomes a warm supporter of

73

missions and will give his life to help advance that cause.

Oh, that God's will for the salvation of all men might be found in each one of us! The glory of God is nothing less than this: His unfathomable love for all who are lost and miserable, His will that they should be saved. When will Christians come to realize that this is their glory, their likeness to God, to allow themselves to be filled with the loving will of God, to let it possess them, devour them? Obedience to all the individual commandments of God, which are expressions of His will, is merely a first step on the path to this higher oneness with the will of God that longs to bless and save.

23

I Am Come to Do Thy Will

> When he said, Sacrifice and offering . . . for sin *thou wouldest not,* neither hadst pleasure therein . . . then said he, Lo, *I come to do thy will,* O God. He taketh away the first that he may establish the second. *By the which will* we are sanctified through the offering of the body of Jesus Christ once for all (Heb. 10:8-10).

David speaks about sacrifices as something God did not want and with which He was not pleased. He had instituted them as a temporary shadow of what He really wanted — the sacrifice of the will to Him. That is why David said, speaking for himself as well as for the Lord Jesus in whom the words would finally attain full meaning: "Lo, I come to do thy will" (see Ps. 40:6-8). In His life and in His death, this is what inspired Him and gave worth to all that He did and suffered. He sought nothing else but to do the will of God.

"By the which will we are sanctified through the offering of the body of Jesus Christ once for all." *Sanctified* is used here in its broadest sense, meaning redeemed, dedicated to God as His possession, indwelt by God and made holy. It refers not so much to the progressive work of sanctification as to its root and its power, the once-for-all rebirth by which we become partakers of power to live a new and holy life. The writer has this in mind when he says, *"By the which will we are sanctified."* That is to say, our sanctification is the will of God, planned by the Father from eternity, accomplished by the Son in time, and now transmitted to us and implanted in us by the Spirit. By this will of God we, having received the Lord Jesus into our hearts as the Executor of that will, are now the sanctified ones.

These words throw a new and glorious light on the work of salvation. They teach three important lessons. They tell us that the doing of God's will is the very nature and strength and purpose of salvation. They tell us that Christian living is characterized and distinguished by this: the doing of God's will. And they tell us that even as our first sanctification rests on Christ's doing the will of God, so our progress in sanctification cannot be accomplished in any other way. Christ, living in us and giving to us, works the will of God in us.

Pause a moment to ponder the last of these lessons. This same Lord Jesus, who was the Executor of the will of God on your behalf on the cross, lives in heaven now, even as He lived on earth, *to carry out that same will of God in you* and bring it to completion. In this you find the answer to the question: Where will I turn to find the wisdom and courage, the joy and strength, to always do the will of God? Only he who gives himself wholeheartedly to do God's will, desiring the indwelling of Christ for that purpose, can fully experience Christ in his heart and can truly say, "Christ liveth in me." On the other hand, only he who can honestly say, "Christ liveth in me," is able to do the will of God always and with joy.

Here lies the great secret, so simple and yet so profound, of the perfecting of the Christian life. A strong desire never for one moment to do anything but what fully accords with the will of God; a deep awareness of our utter inability to do this; a clear insight into the work of Jesus as the one who executed the will of God and now works that will within us; an unwavering confidence that He will accomplish this divine work through the Holy Spirit; accepting Jesus to live in the heart as guide and inspiration; a life of much prayer and of complete dependence, joyful in the certainty that He will do it — these are merely several facets of the great truth: The Lord Jesus came to do the will of God, and in that will we are sanctified.

Oh, Christian, take these words of our Lord and hold them close in your own heart: "Lo, I come to do Thy will, O God!" Make them yours by faith in Jesus Christ, for they express all that He came to do. Welcome Him into your heart as the one who came for that purpose and He Himself will give you the joy of the Holy Spirit, and the doing of God's will will be your chief delight here on earth as well as in heaven.

24

Doing God's Will – the Promise Inherited

> For ye have need of patience, that, *after ye have done the will of God*, ye might receive the promise (Heb. 10:36).

The apostle has spoken of persecutions that Christians were enduring. He tells them that in the midst of these persecutions they need patience to receive the promise. Some in the church had become fainthearted; they were not persevering to the end and thus they were forfeiting the promise. What was that in which they must persevere if they would be counted faithful? They must persevere in *doing God's will*. "You have need of patience, that *after ye have done the will of God*, ye might receive the promise."

There is an important lesson taught here: In a time of trial the Christian must be concerned about only one thing — to remain within the will of God and do it. The one thing most Christians desire in the time of trial is to escape as soon as possible. This may not, however, be of first importance. Rather, the most important thing is to guard against doing even the least thing contrary to the will of God. Many think they ought not to be blamed if they become angry when they are persecuted or if they speak evil of those who mistreat them; the temptation is so strong! But God's Word teaches something different. It sees the Christian as one so completely freed from his own will to do the will of God, so firmly committed in his choice of God's will as his heavenly joy, that he has learned to accept trials as the test of what God can enable him to do.

But isn't that really more than one can expect from anyone, to think first of God's will when trials come? And to always do it? Indeed it is. For that very reason superhuman strength, heavenly grace, is given at such a time. For that very purpose the Lord Jesus came to earth to be an example for us of how a man in most distressing trials sought nothing else but to do the will of God. For that purpose He also went to heaven, to bestow on us His Spirit, His nature, His life, His very self within us, that we, like Him, might do only the will of God in every time of trial. It was *"through the eternal Spirit"* (Heb. 9:14) that He offered Himself to God without spot; through *the selfsame Spirit* He enables us to also offer ourselves. *God's Spirit makes possible what otherwise would be impossible.*

This seems to remind us once again of the great weakness in the church of Christ — men try to live a life in keeping with the will of God apart from the power of the Holy Spirit. They are willing to follow the example of Jesus in some things, even to be conformed to His image, without the power that He gives. It follows automatically that their measure of doing God's will is limited to what seems at least reasonably possible. They fail to realize how impossible it is for a child of God to walk according to God's will unless the heart is entirely in the possession of the Spirit of the Son of God. The first preaching of the gospel was "with the Holy Ghost sent down from heaven" (1 Peter 1:12). With knowledge of the will of God came the strength to do it. To this the church must return.

Dear reader, do not wait for others; begin it yourself. If you simply and wholeheartedly give yourself *to do all the will of God,* you have the right to believe that God accepts your gift and seals it with the Holy Spirit. You must do your part; God will do His. It is only by way of *the will of God* that we can obtain full blessedness, here and hereafter. Do not be afraid to offer yourself *to do all His will,* to be and to bear and to do whatever His will asks. His will is life, love, power, blessedness. Offer your whole self to His will as to the will of your Father; He will give you the Spirit of His Son with power. And, though you may need much endurance and much patience, having done the will of God, you will receive the promise — also the promise of the Holy Spirit in all His fullness.

25

In Order That You May Do His Will, God Works in You

> The God of peace . . . make you perfect in every good
> work *to do His will,* working in you that which is well-
> pleasing in His sight, through Jesus Christ (Heb.
> 13:20,21).

That you may do His will is presented to us here as the
great objective God has in view in saving us. Note that "do
His will" is placed between two thoughts. First, there is
the prayer "The God of peace make you perfect in every
good work." For what purpose? That you may *do His will.*
And how shall this be accomplished? "Working in you
that which is well-pleasing through Jesus Christ." God
Himself would make us perfect in every good work; He
Himself wants to work in us that which pleases Him,
through Jesus Christ — all with this one aim in view: *that
we may do His will.*

Try to grasp the meaning of this deep within your heart.
God's eternal council of grace, God's salvation through
Christ, God's work within us by the Holy Spirit — these

all have but one aim: *that we may do His will.*

To rightly see how closely this is bound up with the work of salvation, notice what is said about God. It is a brief summary of what is taught throughout the letter to the Hebrews about salvation. "The God of peace, that brought again from the dead our Lord Jesus that great Shepherd of the sheep, through the blood of the everlasting covenant, make you perfect . . . to do His will." This is the crown, the fruit, of all that is taught about the covenant and the blood and the exaltation of our Lord. The God who planned and performed it all in Christ is the God who makes you perfect in every good work *in order that you may do His will.*

Note further how certain and sure it is that you will be made capable of doing His will. You need only be still and open your heart to His words "the God of peace . . . make you perfect in every good work, to do His will." Could you ask more? But there is more. Listen to what follows: "working in you that which is well-pleasing in his sight, through Jesus Christ." If God undertakes to do these two things — He Himself making you perfect in every good work and He Himself working in you what is well-pleasing to Him, all so that you may do His will — is there any doubt that you can do it? There simply is no room for doubt. God works it out; you can do it.

But then what is it that has kept me so far from this goal until now? And how shall I begin to go about it, to do all His will? The secret is found in the very simple but meaningful words "yield yourself in faith."

Yield. You have yielded yourself to the Lord, but you did not know that this surrender must include *doing all His will.* Now you begin to realize: God really asks this of me; His will is heaven; His will is pure love; His will is inconceivable bliss. He asks first of all that I yield myself wholly to His divine will; this will then lives within me and works itself out to completion. He does not ask that you fulfill His will as something apart from you and in your own strength. He desires that you surrender yourself, as His possession, to the power of His divine will so that He can work it within you. Won't you do so? Once the living will of God has taken possession of you, and once you have come to truly desire it, the joy will follow and the strength to embrace each part of each command will be there.

Yield in faith. The yielding can be accomplished and confirmed only by faith. But by faith it can be done! For the will of God is not, like the law of Moses, a set of laws that you are not able to keep. No! The will of God is the power that upholds the universe, that brought about salvation, that works all things in all. Yield yourself completely to this perfect will and be assured that when it requires this or that of you, *God Himself will work His will in you.* He will perfect you in every good work, that you may do His will with His strength while He works within you what is well-pleasing to Him. Do not be afraid, but complete your yielding in faith, your total commitment to the will of God. Once you have accepted the will of God in all its heavenly beauty, and love it as the deepest desire of your heart, you will welcome whatever that will may desire or command.

26

If the Lord Will . . .

> For that ye ought to say, *If the Lord will*, we shall live,
> and do this, or that (James 4:15).

Our complete dependence on the will of God is nowhere
more clearly evident than in the fact that we cannot
determine what our life will be even one day ahead, or
even one hour. Yet the accusation against Belshazzar is
still all too applicable to Christians: "The God in whose
hand thy breath is and whose are all thy ways, hast thou
not glorified" (Dan. 5:23). If I am so wholly dependent on
God for every breath I take, it certainly behooves me to
honor Him accordingly. And the more I feel that every
moment of my life is dependent on *the will of God,* the more
keenly aware I will be that my life must be *in accordance
with that will.* This in turn strengthens me in believing that
such oneness is possible, since the same will that upholds
the temporal life must surely care for the spiritual life also.
When we glorify God as the one who holds our very life in
His hand, we are thereby wonderfully encouraged to live
wholly according to His will.

The great sin of our age is that men forget they are creatures, that they have a Creator who has made them and to whom they belong. The amazing power over nature that man has acquired through science has misled him into looking for pleasure and fulfillment in the mastery of creation.

The blessedness and privilege of belonging to a great Creator — such a thought does not occur to them. And Christians are too easily influenced by the spirit of the world around them; they fall short of the continuous dependence on God that is the secret of continuous blessed fellowship with Him. James gives us advice that can be a great help in maintaining the right relationship to God. He teaches us that instead of making plans and saying, "We will go here or there and do this or that" (v. 13), we should cultivate a disposition that says: If the Lord will. . . .

Let us see what kind of blessing we may expect as a result of such a disposition. First of all, it helps us realize that we are living because God wills it, that even the gift of each new day is an act of His will. It is a memorable hour in a person's life when for the first time he fully realizes: *I am here by the will of God;* the eternal God has a plan for me: I am a thought, a project, of the all-wise One. I have a place here, and a work to do, by the will of God, a place no one else can fill. No matter how insignificant I may be, here I am, a living being, one whom God definitely willed to be here. That I am alive here and now is a small part of the perfect will of God.

This is true not only of my life in general, as a whole, as an individual living being in distinction from all others, but also of each detail of my life and every part of my being, outward and inward. When God wills something, He wills it to be good. For whatever He wills, He supplies all that is needed. If it is His will that I live, it is also His will that my life be conformed to His will in every detail and He will give me strength to that end. If I am His child, I may be absolutely sure that He will supply whatever I need to do His will, to live as His child.

A further result will be this: We will learn that *a life wholly dependent* on God's will as its source must also be *wholly conformed* to His will. If something bears the clear stamp: "By the will of God," how can I use it contrary to His will? Surely that which exists by His will, which is strengthened and made holy by His will, ought to be entirely in accordance with His will. As I become more and more childlike in total dependence on God, I will also become more confident, in the assurance of faith, that God will give strength to do His will under any circumstance His will may lead me into. And my choice, to do His will in everything and always, will grow more and more firm and joyful.

The way to such a life we already know. It begins with the humbling discovery that we have fallen short of living within the will of God and the conviction that God can change all this. Its strength lies in acknowledging the greatness of God and choosing His will as the only power that will rule us as well as supply all our need. And as again and again we say, *"If the Lord will,"* we are led into the ever deeper meaning and wider application, for it involves all that we think or do. I would live wholly according to His will. In a twofold way *His will is my life.*

27

Suffering According to the Will of God

For it is better, if *the will of God be so,* that ye suffer for *well-doing,* than for evil-doing (1 Peter 3:17).

For so is *the will of God,* that with *well-doing* ye may put to silence the ignorance of foolish men (1 Peter 2:15).

Wherefore let them that suffer *according to the will of God* commit the keeping of their souls to him in *well-doing,* as unto a faithful Creator (1 Peter 4:19).

Before Peter received the Holy Spirit, he did not realize that suffering must be endured as the will of God. That is why he rebuked the Lord when He spoke of His suffering, and in turn he was rebuked by the words "Get thee behind me, Satan!" It is also why he denied his Lord — he could not understand that he must look on suffering as the will of God. But at Pentecost everything was changed. He no longer feared danger. He rejoiced when he suffered shame for Christ. His letters are filled with this one idea: Through suffering to glory! Let us see what he has to teach us about the will of God in suffering.

Peter teaches us *to see the will of God* in suffering: "If it be the will of God that ye suffer . . ."; "Them that suffer according to the will of God. . . ." The suffering to which he refers was caused by the injustice of fellowmen. That is the kind of suffering that many cannot see as the will of God. But unless you do, you will never learn how to rightly conduct yourself during such suffering. All such suffering, from the intense suffering of Jesus inflicted by Judas and Caiaphas and Pilate down to the little annoyances you may experience from friend or enemy or family, is God's will. Nothing can happen to you apart from the will of God! That men commit such sin is not the will of God, but that you must suffer because of their sin is His will. And your reaction to the suffering will depend entirely on whether you think of it as coming from man or as coming from God. The first will anger you and lead you to sin. The second — that is, if you look upon it as coming from God — will make you forget the one who caused the suffering and bow in submission to God, praying that He will teach you His purpose, trusting that through the suffering He will bless you as well as help you. I would urge you, therefore, first of all to recognize the will of God in your suffering; accept it as a part of His perfect loving will, and it will surely become a blessing.

Peter further teaches us that God wills us to suffer with *well-doing*. The words are found in all three of the above texts. That an evildoer, deserving punishment, should bear suffering patiently requires no special grace, says Peter. Everyone should do that. But to bear suffering patiently when it is unjust, when one has done well, that is God's grace. And it is what God expects of a Christian. It is His will concerning us that when we suffer, we should not be led into sin; rather, while bearing the will of His providence, we should also do the will of His precepts. God's great objective in permitting suffering is that we grow in sanctification, be freed from sin, and be molded to His will. How foolish we are, then, when we allow the suffering that was sent for our sanctification to increase our sinfulness, letting sin take control of us! That is what we do as soon as we forget that suffering is the will of God, instead of bearing it wholeheartedly as His will, and also doing His will. We ought always to suffer "with well-doing." That will stop the mouths of ignorant and foolish ones. They will see, in the way we bear suffering, that we are different from the children of the world. They will ask what enables us to bear suffering that way, and so they will come to know that God is with us, supporting us with His divine love.

If we bear suffering that way, we will also dare to appropriate a third lesson that Peter teaches us: *"to commit the keeping of our souls to him in well-doing as unto a faithful Creator."* He who knows that it is God who allows the suffering dares to commit his soul to Him joyfully as to a faithful Creator. Surely, it is unthinkable that God should lead His child into suffering and not give the strength and the grace to endure it. Would a mother give her sick child medicine and not do all she can to see that the medicine is effective? And would God put a cup of suffering to our lips for healing without watching over us with blessings? Impossible! Rather, it is especially in time of suffering that the Lord reveals His faithfulness. Let us, then, commit our souls to Him as to a faithful Creator.

Do you long, O Christian, to know the will of God? Then by all means do not forget to recognize His will in suffering, in every trial great or small, accepting it with a childlike welcome as *the loving will of your Father!* Make sure, also, that in whatever suffering you may have to bear as the will of God you do His will and you do not sin against Him. And be assured that in all that you may suffer according to His will, you may commit your soul to Him, knowing positively that He, your faithful Creator, will provide all the strength and all the blessing you can ever need.

28

Living According to God's Will

> . . . that he no longer should live the rest of his time in the flesh to the lusts of men, but to *the will of God*. For the time past of our life may suffice us to have wrought *the will of the Gentiles* . . . (1 Peter 4:2,3).

What is the difference between a true Christian and one who is Christian only in name? The first lives *according to the will of God;* he does what God wants him to do. The other lives as the heathen do, according to the will of men. He lives as the world lives and wills what worldly people will. And what is characteristic of the worldly? The Lord told us in His Sermon on the Mount: "Take no thought, saying, What shall we eat? or, What shall we drink? or, Wherewithal shall we be clothed? (For *after all these things do the Gentiles seek.)* . . . But seek ye first the kingdom of God, and His righteousness" (Matt. 6:31-33). Most people, the people of the world, are especially interested in temporal things, in possessions, and in the pleasures of this life. The true Christian puts the kingdom of God and His righteousness first; he seeks the will of God. To him, the invisible, the spiritual, is reality. To him, doing the right and living according to the will of God, full of humility and love and holiness, is much more important than all that the world may offer, and he seeks these more earnestly than anything else.

Alas, there are so many Christians who live according to the will of men and find their pleasure in this present world! They have never given serious thought to the startling difference there is between living according to the will of God and living according to human will, nor have they understood what the difference between a heavenly life and a worldly life is. They do not realize that by nature man lives to satisfy his own will and enjoy the visible things. Apparently they do not know that one who has been born anew ought to live only for the will of God and for His heavenly Kingdom.

Dear reader, we have seen again and again how glorious the will of God is, how necessary it is that we know it and do it, and how blessed it is to be wholly committed to it. I need not speak of that here. But I want to ask you if you have really come to the point where you say to God, "Yes, Lord! *I want to live wholly according to Thy will.*" I am not asking if you already do so. Something must precede the doing — something essential to the beginning of such a life. Right now the question is: Has it become a settled matter between you and God that *you want to live only within and according to His will?* That is a choice any sincere heart can make, a vow that even the weakest can bring to God. You may feel that you can never keep such a vow, but remember — it is not a matter of your own strength. God Himself must work His will within you. Think once more of what we said about Hebrews 13:21. But before He can begin to work His will within you, you must wholeheartedly choose that will for your life and commit yourself to it.

The question is not whether you feel you have the strength to do all of God's will. The question is: Do you truly desire to do it and are you ready to entrust yourself to God to work His will within you? God's will is inseparable from God Himself; He does all things according to the counsel of His will; He Himself will perform all that He wills. But He does so within us only when we offer Him our will to be absorbed in His. When we offer our will sincerely, we can be sure that He will fulfill His will in us. God's will is divine power at work; he who yields to this will, allowing it to work within him, wholeheartedly consenting to it, may depend on God for strength to carry it out.

I am appealing to all, but especially to young Christians, give yourself entirely to live according to the will of God! You must make a decision, a clear-cut choice, by which you commit yourself to the will of God forever. Do it now. Having done so, you may ask God to make known to you whatever He wills for you, and ask Him to reveal to you how you may find strength to do that will. Then, as you kneel before God in quiet meditation and complete trust, you may also thank Him for this glorious certainty: Now God's will will be done in me! You may claim the faithfulness and power and love of God as a pledge that He will work out His will in you. But, whatever happens, hold to your decision as forever unchangeable; consider yourself a committed one, separated to do the will of God in every little thing, never in anything to live or to will according to the will of men. May this thought, this consecration, underlie all your fellowship with God and also all your contacts with the world. The Holy Spirit will confirm you in it.

29

Doing God's Will, the Secret of Steadfastness

> If any man love the world, the love of the Father is not in him.... And the world passeth away, and the lust thereof: but *he that doeth the will of God* abideth for ever (1 John 2:15,17).

Here we again have the two great warring powers contrasted — the world and the will of God. He who loves the world cannot love God. He who loves the world lives according to the will of men. He who loves God lives according to the will of God; he does God's will. Let this be clearly imprinted on our minds: Man is a dependent creature and is guided either by the power of the will of this world or by the power of the will of God. One or the other. Is it clear to you that you are not "of this world"? that you are one whose outstanding characteristic among men on earth and before God in heaven is this — *that you live to do the will of God?*

The blessing that comes from doing the will of God is mentioned in our text: "He that doeth the will of God abideth forever." That is to say, the will of God gives him stability, a steadfastness that remains through time and eternity. Change and decay characterize the world; "the world passeth away, and the lust thereof," all that is desirable in it. That is true of all that is in and of the world, even its religion. Why is it that so many Christians are unstable, forever backsliding? Only because there is still so much of worldly spirit in them; this causes instability. The will of God is eternal and unchangeable, and one who does that will acquires a steadfastness of will and character that keeps him standing. "He shall never be moved."

As we consider this, we are reminded again how important it is to do the will of God. The will of God is the perfect expression of His unseen glory. We cannot see God or know Him directly. How then can we have fellowship with Him? *By doing His will.* All of God's grace revealed in Jesus Christ and all that He does to awaken faith in us is intended only to restore us to our original and glorious state of being like-minded with Him, that our will be one with His. Whenever we keep even one of the least of His commandments, in obedience to Him, or endure suffering in accordance with His will, for His sake, we have made a beginning toward becoming reunited with His will. Then, led by the Spirit, we advance toward fuller knowledge, more wholehearted oneness of will, and more joy in our obedience. Thus we come to find God Himself more and more, for in the measure that we love and do His will, we discover gradually, imperceptibly, what joy there is in being close to Him. Doing the will of God is the sure way to full enjoyment of the rocklike stability that there is in God and that He desires to impart to His children.

Christian, though you do at times enjoy blessing and inspiration, haven't you complained, "But it doesn't last! My innermost life is so unstable and so constantly changing! Show me how to find a life that is not forever wavering and faltering." Well, this is how: "He that doeth the will of God abideth forever." Quite likely you have never before grasped the truth that *doing God's will* is the most important thing in life. You have not understood that this must be your chief desire, the one thing for which you strive every day and every hour, because it is the one purpose for which you were created and for which you were redeemed. You have not known that the Holy Spirit is willing to work within you such a hunger for God's will that doing it becomes your daily bread, your joy, your strength. You have not believed that He gives strength to always do His will. No wonder your life, like that of many others, is so unstable — you have not known the only means for making it stable: *"He that doeth the will of God* abideth forever."

There is only one remedy. Cry to the Lord with the fervent plea that He may open your eyes to see that true Christianity, true following of Christ, is nothing more or less than this: *doing the will of God.* Persist in prayer that He will reveal to you the heavenly beauty and desirability of His will. And as you pray, even before you pray, commit yourself again and again, with unwavering resolve, to do His will, the whole of His will, only His will, in everything, and always. Pray that the Holy Spirit will brand you, as it were, with His mark of ownership: "I am one who lives only to know and do the will of God; I fear only one thing — that I should fail to know and do it." Then you will experience what this means: "He that doeth the will of God abideth forever." Lord God, teach me to do Thy will!

30

Praying According to the Will of God

> And this is the confidence that we have in him, that, if
> we ask anything *according to his will*, he heareth us (1 John
> 5:14).

These words were given by the Spirit of God to fill us
with confidence and assure us that our prayers are being
answered. But for many Christians they are a stumbling
block. How can we be sure, they ask, that our prayers are
according to the will of God?

This is indeed a weighty question. How can I know?
Only by being filled with the knowledge of God's will, in
all wisdom and spiritual understanding! Many Christians
would like to know concerning some particular circumstance if their prayer is according to God's will. They
cannot be sure. The reason is at hand: If I want to know
this for my own satisfaction, while for the rest I have little
interest in knowing or doing the will of God, then God will
not make it known to me. Only if my heart desires to know
and do the will of God *in all things,* and God sees that I

have committed myself to His will, am I capable of knowing if my prayer is according to His will. The Lord Jesus once said, "If any man will to do His will, he shall know of the doctrine" (John 7:17). So you see, *doing* His will precedes knowing! The doing of His will shows that I am not seeking my honor but God's. The doing of His will purifies and sanctifies the mind, making it spiritually receptive to know His will. There must be a strong desire to be filled with the knowledge of the will of God for my whole life; such desire proves that His will is my joy, that I am not merely asking that what I wish may be His will, but that I truly want His will to be my desire and to be fulfilled in me.

The rule then is this: *Live each day wholly committed to the will of God and you will be able to know whether your prayers are according to His will.* God's will is one great whole. Accept it in its completeness, love and acknowledge it in each commandment and every experience that comes to you. Then, because you are living within His will, you will know how to pray according to His will. Oh, the will of God is not an iron bar that we may hope to bend here and there by our pleadings and supplications. No, the will of God is His perfect love. Live within it, let your will be captivated by it and filled with it; then you will learn to will what He wills and His Spirit will tell you that your prayers are being answered. Not only is God's will a whole; your life is also one whole. And of that life prayer is but a small part. As your life is, so will your prayers be; they are not a matter of isolated thoughts and desires. Therefore — let me say it once again — the secret of knowing whether your prayer is according to the will of God is this: *Only one who lives according to the will of God knows how to pray according to the will of God.*

Let us look at this from a different angle. The pressing question is: Which is more important, your desire or the will of God? If the first looms more important, and if because you are very eager to have your request granted you hope it may be the will of God, then you are not likely to arrive at any certainty about it. But as soon as you have learned to accept the will of God, which is done in heaven, as your supreme joy and only aim in life, so that it is more important than your desire, then the Spirit of God will teach you to know God's will.

Christian, whether we speak of God's will in His commandments or in our prayers, whether done in heaven above or on earth beneath, it all comes down to this: We must first of all and above all give ourselves, commit ourselves, wholly to that will. The will of God is His love, His glory, His power. Need we hesitate to give ourselves into His hands, into His control? The Word has opened before you the glorious prospect of a heart so filled with the mind and the Spirit of God that prayers will rise from your heart that you know with certainty are according to the will of God. God's will will become your inner life, and as intercessor you will find confidence and assurance that your prayer is according to the will of God.

Lord God, teach Thy people to see the heavenly glory of Thy will, to know, love, do, and trust that will. Yes, Lord, teach them to live wholly within that will. Then they will have the blessed experience of praying according to the will of God and knowing that their prayers are answered.

31

Worship the God by Whose Will All Things Exist

The four and twenty elders . . . cast their crowns before the throne, saying, Thou art worthy, O Lord, to receive glory and honour and power: for thou hast created all things, and for thy pleasure [*by thy will*]* they are and were created (Rev. 4:10,11).

Here, where Scripture last mentions the will of God, it is associated with two very exalted concepts. By His will all things were created; His will is the origin of all and upholds all; everything has emanated from the strength of His will. And it is because He is the God by whose will all things exist that He is accorded worship in heaven. The more we realize that our God is the God by whom and through whom and to whom all things are, the more we will honor and glorify Him. Because all things exist by the will of God alone, so that nothing can have being except by Him, He alone is worthy to receive the glory, the honor,

---

* Most versions, including the Dutch, have the phrase *by thy will*.

and the praise to all eternity. O my soul, try to fathom what this means: All things exist by the will of God. Ponder it till your heart is filled with the exalted glory of it and you lose yourself in wonder and worship.

"All things exist by Thy will" — what a revelation of what God is! Only He has life in Himself. All life in creation around us, all goodness and all joy, came by Him. And this is the wonder of His love that all that He has, He has for His creatures. He brought them forth to be partakers of His goodness and His blessedness, and He works in them all that they are and must be. Everything in the universe, all that is beautiful in nature, all that is amazing in creation around us and in man himself, has its origin in, and is dependent on, the will of God. In everything we see His power and wisdom. Glorious will of God!

That glory is especially evident in redemption, the restoration of man to his first estate. All that has been wrought through Christ, all that is being done through Him now, whatever is good or lovely or strong in the church or in one of God's children — all is from God, all has come by His will. Glorious will of God!

When we reflect on all this, we need not ask, "Is this God worthy of all honor and praise?" If we but had eyes and hearts to know this God as we ought, if the Holy Spirit would grant us for just one moment an insight into the full meaning of the statement *All things are by Thy will alone,* our hearts would respond with rejoicing: *Therefore may all things be to Thy honor alone!* To Him be the glory and the honor and the power!

We are nearing the end of our meditations. Let us summarize, then, by recalling what we ought to ask of God in prayer in order that we may be taught by His Spirit.

Pray much that your eyes and your heart may be enlightened so that you may see God's will as His eternal council of love concerning us as His children — our creation, redemption, sanctification, and glorification. Pray that He will enable you to see that in all of this He has prepared indescribable blessedness for us on earth, and that your great task is to be in complete harmony with that will day by day.

Pray to be filled with the knowledge of His will in all wisdom and spiritual understanding, so that in everything, even the minor daily events, you may know what God's will is for you. Do not rest until you know that you are standing steadfast in His will because God Himself is working in you that which is well-pleasing to Him.

And pray especially that Jesus Christ may so dwell in you and that by faith you may have such a lively conviction of His presence that you are always certain He is at work within you and will continue that work.

Then you will come to understand and experience what it means that all things are by the will of God, because it is the triune God — the Father through the Son and the Spirit — who is continually working His own will in you. And your heart will join the heavenly beings in their worship: Thou, Lord, art worthy to receive the glory and the honor and the power, for all things are by Thy will! Then you will recognize God's will as His highest glory, the revelation of His perfection and His love. Then your life will be permeated with heavenly joy, for you will realize that you are one in whom God's will is being fulfilled, one through whom He is being glorified, one in whom the Triune God Himself and His will will be reflected and revealed forever.

May that be life for each one of us, by God's grace.

O my God, I bow humbly before Thee in worship, before Thee the All-glorious, by whose will all things are. Without Thee there is nothing good or true. In Thy will all that is holy and glorious has its being. Thou art worthy to receive — and my soul would bring to Thee — all glory and honor and power.

I pray Thee, fill my heart with the knowledge of Thy will — Thy will in the eternal council, in upholding and controlling all things, in the glorious work of redemption, in its commandments for my daily life, in its revelation in Christ Jesus. Oh, teach me so to know and love Thy will that the longing to do Thy will may be greater than any other desire of my life.

I pray Thee, teach me to know Christ better as the one who accomplished all Thy will and the One to whom Thou hast given the charge to work that will within me. Strengthen my faith, that I may gladly and without any reservation entrust myself to Him completely.

Father, let Thy will be done in me, here on earth, even as it is done in heaven. Even so, may my heart and my life be filled with the will of my God, with Thy Son who came to do Thy will, and with heaven, which is wherever Thy will is. Then my daily song will be: Thou art worthy to receive the glory and the honor and the power!

Amen.